Steve Clayton

TALKING HEADS

A BIOGRAPHY BY JEROME DAVIS

GW00771755

Omnibus Press
London/New York/Sydney/Cologne

Edited by Mark Rowland. Consulting Editor *Musician* Magazine
ISBN 0-7119-1116-9
Order No. OP 44338

Exclusive distributors:
Book Sales Limited
8/9 Frith Street, London W1V 5TZ, UK.

Omnibus Press
GPO Box 3304, Sydney,
NSW 2001, Australia.
To the Music Trade only:
Music Sales Limited
8/9 Frith Street, London W1V 5TZ, UK.
Printed in Britain by
The Anchor Press Limited, Tiptree, Essex.

TO VIC GARBARINI

ACKNOWLEDGMENTS

We would like to thank the following people for their cooperation and support in the creation of this book: Bob Babbitt, Toni Basil, Karen Berg, Ed Bicknell, Tony Bongiovi, Ken Braun, David Breskin, David Brown, Janis Bultman, Rudy Cheeks, Mary Clarke, Paul Cummins, Jamie Dalglish, Brian Eno, Tommy (Ramone) Erdelyi, Danny Fields, Carol Fonde, Stephanie Franklin, Deborah Frost, Steve Futterman, Frank Gallagher, Naomi Reichbart Gittler, Dan Gosch, David Hansen, Nona Hendryx, Stan Hertzman, John Illsley, Scott Isler, Busta Jones, Lenny Kaye, Mark Kehoe, Kevin Kearney, Melissa Kearney, David Knopfler, Mark Knopfler, Andrea Kovacs, Hilly Krystal, Karen Moss, Elliott Murphy, Matt Murphy, Elisa Petrini, Jill Priest, Lance Quinn, Dee Dee Ramone, Ira Robbins, Charles Rocket, Donna Russo, Zoe Rygh, Andy Schwartz, Jeff Shore, Rhonda Shore, Fred Smith, Steve Stanley, Ed Stasium, Seymour Stein, Anthea Norman Taylor, Diane Terenana, Jeff Turtletaub, Mark Wagner, Vicki Wickham, Bernie Worrell, Michael Yockel, Chip Young, Wayne Zieve, Marie Zuberbuehler. And to Galen Brandt, for providing transcripts of her early interviews with the group.

Also, thanks to our coeditors, Mark Rowland and Patty Romanowski, as well as to our editor at Random House, Erroll McDonald, and Nancy Pittman. And to Bill Flanagan, whose efforts and vision made this book possible.

INTRODUCTION

Some people like rock & roll, some people hate it, and some people never think about it at all. But in rock's three decades, the most annoying group of rock fans has been the apologists, who try to make excuses for rock music. At the beginning those excuses took the form of comparisons, with those guilty of committing moral offenses held up as examples of how bad rock could be. By some strange leap of logic, someone or something deemed not so bad would become "acceptable." To wit: "That Jerry Lee Lewis is a vulgar pig, but Pat Boone is a nice boy; not all rock & roll is bad."

By the mid-sixties the apologists felt compelled to offer some proof that rock's intellect—though questionable—did indeed exist. "That Elvis Presley may be a cretin," went the new "logic," "but Bob Dylan is like a poet, and the Beatles are witty; not all rock & roll is moronic."

These arguments cut some ice with sensitive high school English teachers and liberal parents, but it seemed the most backhanded of compliments to those who believed that rock & roll did not need to be morally upright or especially intelligent—and it certainly did not need to be excused.

In the eighties Talking Heads became the rock band for people who considered themselves too good—or too smart —to rock. The old apologist thought pattern, in eighties' vernacular, ran something like: "Those slobs on MTV may be garish and obvious, but Talking Heads are ironic intellectuals; not all rock & roll is vulgar."

As singer, songwriter, and—in the minds of everyone except, perhaps, the other band members—leader of Talking Heads, David Byrne was the magnet for most of the praise and attention. Byrne did nothing to discourage the notion that he was a deep thinker in a field believed to be overrun by cavemen. The apologists, all of whom believe that other art forms are legitimate in a way rock & roll is not, genuflected with joy when Byrne wrote music that was choreographed by Twyla Tharp (*The Catherine Wheel*); wrote lyrics for tunes by a serious contemporary composer (Philip Glass); came up with music for *The Knee Plays* (a segment of Robert Wilson's theater piece *The CIVIL warS*); and worked with director Jonathan Demme on the Talking Heads movie *Stop Making Sense*, which won a 1984 best documentary award from the National Society of Film Critics.

You'd think, to hear apologists tell it, that Byrne had done the dancing, acted in the play, and directed the film. But in each case, Byrne stuck to his role as recording artist and songwriter. He was graced by association, in the same way that Leonard Cohen and Jim Carroll were supposed to be better rock songwriters because they were *real* poets first (that is, published in books), or Kris Kristofferson because he was a Rhodes scholar, or Bob Dylan because he had hung out with real poets like Allen Ginsberg. The true rock fan, on the other hand, would argue that Dylan was a greater artist than Ginsberg anyway.

David Byrne may well be an intellectual. Certainly he has refined tastes. But to appreciate art does not make one an artist. The best case for Byrne's status as an artist can be made from the good rock & roll songs he has written: "Life during Wartime," "Girlfriend Is Better," "Burning Down the House." Just as it's wrong to cast Byrne as a Renaissance man, it's wrong to give in to the peculiarly American temptation to argue Talking Heads' legitimacy on the basis of their having been the "first" or the "biggest" of anything. Their merits are more subtle than that. Talking Heads have been a consistently original and unusually enjoyable band. Their story is interesting for the singularity of the personalities involved and for their very American success story.

Yet, while some of their records are very good, their music has not had an enormous impact on rock & roll. It's not just that the Beatles and David Bowie have been more influential; it's that Van Morrison and Jimmy Page have been more influential.

Talking Heads did not, as some of their more ardent enthusiasts claim, invent New Wave. They were part of a tradition at least as old as the Velvet Underground. But of all the underground bands to emerge from New York City in the seventies—the Ramones, Patti Smith Group, Blondie, Television, and all the arcane offshoots—only Talking Heads went the distance. The Ramones hung on as long, but the Ramones never reached a wide audience. Blondie reached a wide audience but couldn't hang on.

The Talking Heads are often credited with innovations made by Lou Reed and the Velvet Underground a decade before. In fact, there are many parallels between the two New York bands. Each was a quartet that included a woman in the rhythm section (drummer Maureen Tucker of the Velvets, bassist Tina Weymouth in the Heads). Both bands were described as "minimalist," for they played sparsely. Both had singers/guitarists/songwriters who sang their unorthodox lyrics in what were not conventionally considered "good" voices; both leaders loved black pop music but sounded purely white; both bands included one "real" musician (John Cale of the Velvets, Jerry Harrison of the Heads); both were associated with the lower Manhattan art scene, where they both found inspiration. Andy Warhol was the Velvets' patron, and later Byrne would be one of Warhol's fans. Finally, a full decade later, the Velvets' Lou Reed and John Cale were early supporters of the Heads.

All of this is stated early to get out of the way the inaccurate claims that have been made for Talking Heads, claims that form a web of myth around them. The Talking Heads' legitimacy does not come so much from their having been the first at much of anything, as from doing what they do so well.

To the same degree that David Byrne is the public face of Talking Heads, the story of the band is largely the biography of David Byrne. For ten years, Byrne had been a bundle of talent and ideas, with no sense of how to apply his gifts. From the ages of twelve to twenty-two, Byrne wandered through a series of changes, diversions, and wrong turns on his way to finding a method for his special madness. He knew that he wanted to *become* an art project, to animate a created character people would believe was the real David Byrne, but he had no idea how to do it. Then, from twenty-two to thirty-two, Byrne threw himself into Talking Heads, created a remarkably successful career, and, ultimately, grew past the need to do so.

The big difference between those two decades was Tina Weymouth, and it is here that Byrne's life and the life of the Talking Heads become inextricably intertwined. For Tina Weymouth was a woman as focused and ambitious as Byrne was rudderless. Whether by luck or by design, the combination of Byrne's creativity and Weymouth's very American go-getter tenacity fueled an extraordinary entity, a rock band capable of simultaneously and consistently expanding their artistic reputation and their bank accounts.

Tina Weymouth was an admiral's daughter; her husband, Heads drummer Chris Frantz, a general's son. The dichotomy in Talking Heads was between the all-American, success-oriented values of the couple's tradition and the art-for-art's sake, politically liberal background shared by Byrne and keyboard player Jerry Harrison. Weymouth and her husband gave Byrne a practical vehicle through which to work. It seems very likely that if David Byrne had never met them, no one would know who David Byrne was.

The story of Talking Heads is also the story of Tina Weymouth's use of power—how she got it and how she held on to it when it was threatened. David Byrne had a lifelong tradition of leaving people behind; Tina refused to be left. Somehow, when all the growing pains were over, both sides came out on top. Byrne had gained entrée into intellectual circles, public acceptance, and whatever personal gratification an artist derives from acclaim. Tina had emerged wealthy and famous, a winner in the American sweepstakes. And Talking Heads had become a great American band.

No other band in recent memory has matched the Heads' bilevel astuteness: they were as artistically directed as they were career-minded. Talking Heads have promoted the idea that they stumbled on their vocation almost by accident, that they just wanted to play music and went to CBGB because it was the club nearest their Lower East Side home. The implication is that they hardly noticed the fans and media appear. The more one looks into it, though, the more one discovers how carefully planned the group's career has been. Here is that story. And if their manipulation is off-putting, their music is still mighty impressive.

"There's a streak of defiance in David Byrne," Tina Weymouth once observed. "He hates anything that's clichéd in modern life. When he walks, he's always stumbling—he's nervous and so he shows that he's nervous, because that's not a cliché. And when he sits down in a chair, he'll sit down in an unusual way, just because he wants to be an individual."

That commitment to individualism is more than apparent in David Byrne's contributions to music, film, and art, most notably as the guiding force behind Talking Heads, considered by many to be the best American band of the past decade. It is a spirit that links him to pop-culture icons from Dean to Kerouac to Brando to Dylan to Lou Reed. Byrne has always been notably recalcitrant about providing details of his early childhood, inviting speculation that his family circumstances were unusually grim or austere. In fact, David Byrne, born in 1952 and a teenager during the popular-music upheavals of the sixties, grew up in circumstances closer to a hippie's dream.

Byrne's parents are from Scotland. They'd emigrated a few years after David was born and made their home in a planned community called Arbutus, in Baltimore County, Maryland, where David and his younger sister Celia grew up. Byrne's father was an electronics whiz for Westinghouse, who, according to family legend, once fixed a submarine with a coat hanger. His mother returned to school during the sixties and upon graduation worked with retarded children.

Byrne's parents were Quakers who were active in the peace and environmental movements before such activities became fashionable, and whose attitudes remained considerably more open than many of their peers'. "They were progressive people," recalled Mark Kehoe, who met Byrne as a teen in Baltimore. "They were always into folk music. They certainly weren't your normal 'Get a haircut! Get a job!' kind of parents."

Mary Clarke, a former girlfriend of Byrne's, maintains that Byrne's parents "instilled really good values, kind of liberal Democrat. Maybe more radical than that."

"They were very, very wonderful," recalled Michael Yockel, who befriended David in high school. "They weren't part of the whole nouveau-chic/late-sixties/middle-aged-people-getting-interested-in-issues. It was very genuine, and they remain that way today. They listened to a lot of folk music, Scottish music. They were always interested in stuff David and I were listening to as well. They were extremely unusual in a great way."

David's relationship with his younger sister was somewhat less idyllic, if more predictable. Kehoe describes their sibling conflicts: "They'd have horrible arguments. He'd scream, 'Shut up, Celia!' She'd go, 'Shut up you . . . you ugly face!' "

The Byrne household boasted its share of eccentricities. Each morning, Kehoe recalls, David's parents would get up and turn on the radio, the television, the alarm clocks. "Everything would be on full blast and everyone would be running around." The Byrne house also sheltered a virtual archive of electric teapots, which would harmonize with the other appliances. "Sometimes they were all going at once."

Along with the teapots, the Byrnes had lots of tea cozies,

padded cloth caps that fit over the kettles, which Kehoe says that he and David wore as hats: "They made us look like Shriners."

By the time David entered seventh grade at Arbutus Junior High, he was acquiring a reputation as a bit of an oddball.

"In terms of what was cool then, I would have to characterize David as pretty nerdy," said Michael Yockel. But during the course of junior high, Byrne and Yockel made "a conscious effort to be more hip, more cool, and certainly more artistic than the rest of the kids. We set ourselves apart from the jocks." They started wearing paisley shirts, in the Mod fashion of the time, and David began playing guitar. He soon started his first band, a Top 40 outfit called the Revelations. The Revelations played at local CYO (Catholic Youth Organization) gatherings, lost a junior high battle of the bands, and generally bobbed along in the deep wide ocean of sixties garage bands. "We played in people's basements and at sock hops," Byrne would later recall. "Our big song was 'The Last Time.'"

David was a good student—honors classes—but didn't always apply himself to schoolwork. At Lansdowne High School, however, his interest in music, and especially art, expanded. The art classes were conventional, Yockel observes, but within that framework David's work stood out. "He sculpted this long, gaunt white figure, kind of like Abraham Lincoln. He made an African mask, a lot of paintings. David's parents' house is, to this day, filled with all his artwork, dating back to junior high school."

Lansdowne was a relatively conservative, middle-class high school in the southwestern part of Baltimore County, with a restrictive dress code. So Yockel and Byrne were more likely to stand out there than in the more liberal suburbs to the north. Though their hair bordered on long, according to

Yockel, "It was Peter and Gordon–type long hair, not Blue
Cheer–type long hair."

During high school David hung up his rock & roll shoes.
He began giving solo folk performances at a coffeehouse at
the nearby University of Maryland.

"He was doing songs like 'Barabajagal' by Donovan,"
Yockel chuckled. "He did 'Desolation Row' by Dylan,
which was quite an undertaking—sixteen minutes or whatever it was. His singing voice was somewhat Dylanesque,
kind of nasal—but if you're doing a solo folkie thing, you
adopt a Dylanesque twang almost by default.

"He was quite popular, especially among this group of
high school friends that was sort of the nascent hippie
group: the few kids who were smoking grass." But Byrne and
Yockel remained on the periphery, hanging out and smoking
grass on irregular occasions. "David was never particularly
interested in drugs," Yockel explained, "but the hippies
were sympathetic to us musically and sort of philosophically.

"David never expressed anything specific about wanting
to make it. I think he had a vague yearning to succeed in
the arts. One thing he certainly didn't want to do was get
a regular job. I think he wanted to be popular on stage, and
I guess that's synonymous with being a rock star."

David had a big tape recorder, on which he tracked himself while playing guitar, harmonica, ukulele, and any of
several other instruments, while Yockel banged along on
"whatever was handy." Yockel recalls Byrne's tastes veering
toward Joni Mitchell. Byrne's oft-heralded fascination with
black pop and African rhythms was still in its early stage.

"I don't think he listened to any more black music than
what was popular on the radio: the Temptations, the Four
Tops. Later he listened to the Persuasions album, *We Came
to Play*. He wasn't listening to anything like Parliament/
Funkadelic."

Michael had a girlfriend named Wendy Jenkins whom, in teenage fashion, he later abandoned for her best friend. One day in eleventh grade, David telephoned and started hemming and hawing. "He was really beating around the bush," Yockel recalled. "Finally I said, 'What's on your mind?'

" 'Do you mind,' David asked, 'if I go out with Wendy?'

" 'Oh no," I said. "Please, be my guest.' "

So the two couples, best friends, began spending all their time together.

"I think David and Wendy went out for three years. It was sort of tempestuous. David wasn't obsequious, but he bent more than he wanted to. She always wanted to have her way and he pretty much relented."

David would pedal his bicycle a great distance to Wendy's house. This exercise built up his leg muscles to the point that the otherwise unathletic teenager became one of the fastest runners in gym class. But strong leg muscles cut little ice with Wendy's parents.

"They thought David was really weird," Yockel said. "Everybody else got their drivers' licenses as soon as they were sixteen. David didn't. I suppose Wendy's parents thought that was aberrant behavior."

Whether buoyed by love, by school spirit, or by a mischievous streak, David made another stab at getting into the secondary-school swing. He ran for president of the student council, recruiting Yockel as campaign manager.

"It was a loose anarchy party," Yockel explained. "There was an assembly, and each candidate for office got on stage and gave a two- or three-minute speech about what they stood for. David got up there and explained that he wanted to abolish parliamentary procedure, just have a sort of freeform student council. Well, that caused quite a stir among the faculty and administration. Most of the kids had no idea what he was talking about."

Byrne himself remembers running on a platform "to get the jukebox back in the cafeteria and eliminate faculty advisers. I came pretty close," he said. "But I never won."

Yockel's recollection is slightly different. "He got about two votes. One from me and one from Wendy."

Still, Yockel found redemption in David's failed crusade: "He did some incredible posters—real thin lines of white paint on black poster board. They were slung all over the school. Everybody else's posters were done in big block letters: VOTE FOR BOB. David's were quite distinctive by comparison."

If young Byrne could not win the hearts and minds of his colleagues with politics, he could make a typically idiosyncratic stab at wowing them with music. At the senior talent show, David sang old standards like "Down by the Old Mill Stream," accompanying himself on a ukulele. "It was not unlike Tiny Tim, although he didn't have Tiny Tim's physical shtick," Yockel observed. The audience was, however, "dumbstruck"—at least initially. "At first they were laughing. But by the end he'd won a lot of them over."

Following graduation, David got a job as a Good Humor man, peddling ice cream around the neighborhood in a white uniform and cap. This gave him a little money with which to woo Wendy, whose parents remained unimpressed. He told friends he had been accepted at both MIT —his father's flair for electronics was perhaps hereditary— and at the Rhode Island School of Design, a prestigious Providence art college with a slightly bohemian reputation. He chose RISD.

Jeff Turtletaub met David at the beginning of Byrne's freshman year: "Some people were sitting in a room playing guitar. Then David got the guitar and sang, 'Please, Mister Postman.' It was pretty good and pretty different. He had a certain rhythm. David had a beard and looked like a remnant of The Band or a Civil War veteran."

Byrne's first encounter with RISD, the environment that would eventually spawn Talking Heads, turned out to be a brief one. His romance with Wendy Jenkins was still tugging him out of his natural orbit. The following spring, Wendy joined a communal farm in Kentucky; David joined too. The farm community, mostly Baltimore exiles, numbered between twelve and seventeen, including David Brown, whose brother, Jim, owned the place.

"He had a short beard and real, real short hair," said Brown of Byrne. "I think he had just gotten out of his hippie phase. I don't think David was looking for anything or attempting to get anything out of [the farm]. He was just marking time."

Playing music was a big part of life on the Kentucky homestead and naturally Byrne joined in. However, Brown's recollections of their musical endeavors seem partly suspect.

"If you had to describe [our music], I'd say it would be jazz. There would be several guys playing guitars, my brother or I would play drums, and David would play the sax. He was very good."

Informed that Byrne does not play sax in Talking Heads —that no one, in fact, had ever seen any evidence or ever heard any indication that he ever played sax, Brown said, "No? Well, he was great. I thought he had a great future as a saxophonist."

After a few months, Brown returned to Baltimore, where he began doing primate research, studying communication with monkeys. Shortly thereafter, Byrne left the commune and stayed with Brown for a few weeks while searching for a place to live. "He got along better with my research animals than anyone before ever had," Brown said. "There was no problem with him relating with the monkeys. They loved him. David could communicate nonverbally better than most people. He became best friends with a female named Jerome. Couldn't separate the two of them."

Mark Kehoe and David Byrne were best friends in Baltimore, best friends in Providence—best friends until Byrne became famous with Talking Heads. For much of their time together, Kehoe seems to have played a beatnik Huck Finn to Byrne's Tom Sawyer. Another analogy offered was Byrne as Jack Kerouac to Kehoe's Neal Cassady. But while Kerouac idealized his unstrung hero in a novel, Byrne incorporated what was wild in Kehoe into a public persona that came to be identified as David Byrne. Cassady was finally immortalized, while Kehoe—at least, to hear his partisans tell it—was absorbed and then abandoned.

Kehoe, who was from New Jersey, was studying art at Baltimore's Maryland Institute, College of Art, in 1971. His girlfriend lived in Providence. Kehoe often hitchhiked back and forth from Baltimore to see her.

"People kept saying, 'You have to meet David!' 'You must meet David!' " Kehoe recalled. "I was saying, 'Who is this guy? I don't care.' Finally I got a letter from him saying, 'Coming to school in Baltimore / I have no place to live / These people told me to write you a letter.' I had rented a whole floor of a house, so I said, 'Sure.' "

Well, at least Kehoe *thought* he had rented a whole floor: It turned out that during the summer, between the time the deal was struck and the time Kehoe was to move in, the landlord sold the spacious house to an owner unwilling to honor old commitments. When September came, Kehoe found himself with only a single, tiny room and David Byrne as his unknown roommate.

"We lived uncomfortably in this little room," Kehoe explained. "We had to become friends. We went through a series of really terrible apartments together. The first one had a million cockroaches. Once I went downstairs in the middle of the night and the floor was an undulating carpet of roaches. They were everywhere.

"The house was in a bad neighborhood. There were wild dogs in the alley out back. They used to run up and down the alleys all night long. They'd snatch babies out of backyards and eat them."

Kehoe recalls that Byrne liked to play songs by the Beatles on acoustic guitar. Kehoe hated the Beatles, however. They did share an affinity with Smokey Robinson and with James Brown, whose funk-oriented dance riffs and layered rhythmic attacks eventually found their reflection on such Talking Heads albums as *Remain in Light.* "We were very much into the weirder James Brown albums," says Kehoe. "For a while, for every record he put out with him singing, James Brown also put out a record of just music. We would get a lot of those instrumental records. David and I had both come from high schools where it was very uncool to like black music. And we had similar tastes. In the sixties a lot of R&B records that never broke in New York were hits in Baltimore and Philadelphia. Baltimore was such a black town. It's not Diahann Carroll on *Dynasty* black. It's people hustling for a living on the lowest level."

Byrne's other musical favorites included records as diverse as the Ventures and Balinese monkey chants. He'd also borrow albums of electronic music and old Folkways records from the local library. Some of this apparent eclecticism was a reflection of Byrne's upbringing: folk music and electronics were Byrne family absorptions.

"I would say he always wanted to be famous," Kehoe observed. "When I first met David, he would write these weird, sort of free-form poems. A lot of them were about how he wanted to be famous." Of course, a desire for fame, especially among adolescents, isn't so unusual in postwar America. Fame redeems the oddball, and if Byrne's upbringing qualified him as a bit unusual, ninety percent of all teenagers probably feel the same way. But only a few do something about it.

Monkey chants and poetry aside, Byrne and Kehoe were allegedly in Baltimore to study art. The Maryland Institute, where they were enrolled, placed emphasis on formal technique. To Kehoe, the space between Maryland Institute and RISD, the space between photorealism and abstract art, reflected a class difference. RISD was a place where children of the elite indulged their inspirations. Maryland was where middle-class kids learned which kinds of paint to use and how to render accurately.

One day Kehoe met David carrying a painting he had just done in class, a realistic representation of playing cards. "Why are you doing that?" Kehoe demanded.

"Well," David replied, "I don't know." Kehoe insisted such craftsmanship was a waste of time.

Sparked by Kehoe's antiacademic fire, Byrne's old passion for dada soon started smoking. He taped his clothes, including his underwear, onto one of the walls at school, an artistic statement that shocked rather than amused many of his staid peers.

Fellow art student Kevin Kearney described Byrne and Kehoe as "definitely different." "They weren't as interested in art as a lot of other people there. They were interested in various media, primarily music. David, I think, was a very serious musician. He was certainly more stable, at least on the surface. Mark was more overtly flamboyant, crazy."

As Byrne and Kehoe became closer, they attended class less frequently. They'd hitchhike to Washington for a change of pace, or to Providence to visit friends. At first the duo would depart on a Thursday and come back on a Tuesday, says Kehoe. "Then we started leaving on Wednesday and coming back the next Wednesday." After their second year, both got jobs: David in a bar and Kehoe in the public market, chopping and frying chickens.

When life got too funky, Byrne and Kehoe would visit

their parents. David's liberal folks were preferred; they didn't protest if the boys smelled. But when passing through New Jersey on a hitchhike, the pair would sometimes scrounge a meal from Kehoe's less openminded mom and dad. "My mother would meet us at the door with two robes," Kehoe said. "She'd say, 'Get down in that basement and both of you strip down! I'm washing your clothes!' "

When Melissa Kearney was fourteen years old, her older brother brought his art school friend home to dinner. "David seemed almost like a Celtic mystic to me when I first met him," Melissa recalled. "David is not religious, but he is very tied with something spiritual. He is Scottish and I see that as very much an influence. He's very driven by his ideas and creativity. He was a charming fellow despite his very European hygiene habits.

"He was very quiet and talked in little short, breathy sentences. He . . . talked like . . . this. [He still does.] Kind of staccato, short phrases, half-thoughts. But I always understood him."

Melissa began hanging around with Byrne and Kehoe. Her perspective on their artistic abilities was tempered by what the bohemians would undoubtedly have dismissed as a Maryland Institute prejudice. "David was a horrible artist," Melissa said. "He was the worst. But I grew up around classical painters. His big thing was strange drawings of dogs with Contact paper; he could render a dog well. I'm sure if he'd continued as a conceptual artist he would have been successful, but as a classical drawer I didn't think he had it."

Byrne's next creative kick was taking Polaroid photos. He bought a camera and started clicking away at everything in sight. "He wasn't even good at taking Polaroid pictures," Melissa said. "The more fuzzy they were, the more he liked them."

Once, when Melissa took a trip across the country, Byrne

convinced her to snap Polaroids of median strips the whole way. "We all understood," Melissa explained, "that this was a great thing to do." It takes no great leap of the imagination to suppose that Byrne might have been having a little sport with his fourteen-year-old sidekick.

The one Maryland Institute student who vibrated on Byrne and Kehoe's wavelength was a New Yorker named Naomi Reichbart, a self-described "real painter." Naomi talked like Cyndi Lauper, and, while her oddball sensibility matched Byrne's and Kehoe's, she had a down-to-earth side that sometimes made her impatient with their smart-ass cynicism.

"David was always sort of selfish," said Naomi. "He had this act of not being aware of other people's feelings. I still haven't figured out how much of it was real and how much wasn't. That shtick was a way to get out of having to face things, having to face other people's unhappiness or something he did wrong."

Still, in school, Naomi said, she, Byrne, and Kehoe understood one another without saying anything. Once Byrne and Kehoe invited her over to their house for dinner. David made potato soup and cornbread, the latter served implanted with a candle. Naomi brought a cake.

By this time, Byrne had taken up the fiddle and soon decided that his playing deserved a public forum. Kehoe played accordion, and the two of them started performing on street corners. David sang. They called themselves Bizadi, a nonsense word from Byrne's teenage years.

"We did the oldest old standards," Kehoe said. "And we did 'Woolly Bully,' 'Double Shot of My Baby's Love,' '96 Tears.' Little kids would come up to us and say, 'Can you play "Shaft"?' We couldn't play 'Shaft.' "

Bizadi initially performed for people waiting in lines outside theaters; eventually they became rather popular.

They were invited to perform at art gallery openings and even played a concert in a theater. Kehoe would lie on his back or stand on one leg playing accordion. Sometimes they'd perform in the dark; Kehoe would put candles on his accordion, while David secured a candle to the bow of his violin.

By this time Naomi and Kehoe had fallen in love, but she sometimes found her dander rising over Bizadi's more self-indulgent exhibitions. At one show, Kehoe and Byrne were soaring and squeezing their way through "Pennies from Heaven" when Byrne produced a dead fish wrapped in aluminum foil. He put it down on the stage and stamped on it. Then Kehoe stamped on it. Then Byrne. Then Kehoe again. Aghast, Naomi climbed to her feet and, in front of the audience, screamed, "That's stupid! You're so stupid!"

Byrne and Kehoe were like men struck. Mark put down his accordion and left the stage. Byrne just stood there, not knowing what to do. But such moments were only occasional disruptions in their otherwise tranquil lives.

"I remember taking long walks in the snow," Naomi said. "We'd just laugh and stuff. We didn't do too much, but we used to have fun no matter what we did."

One habit Naomi, Byrne, and Kehoe had was crediting all things unusual to nuclear weapons. "Oh, it's cold today," one would note.

"Must be because of the atom bomb," another would reply.

"We never went to bars," Kehoe explained. "When I grew up, in the hippie era, you just never drank. It was completely out. We'd just kind of wander around taking pictures, talk, go to movies. Once we went up to the radio station near the school. The disc jockey had seen us playing on the street, so we brought in our instruments and were on the radio for ten minutes, playing and telling bad jokes."

They bought thrift store clothes and made an impression walking around Baltimore in long coats and beards.

"There were dares," Kehoe explained. "But we'd never say, 'I dare you.' We'd say, 'Why don't you walk on the railing of that bridge?' 'Okay, I'll do it.' We were always walking around. We were like little kids. Once we smoked cigars from the gutter. 'See those two cigar butts?' 'Sure, I'll do it.' We used to put pennies on the train track so Lincoln's face got stretched out."

"I guess David's still the same. He's a weird guy. When you're friends with him, he's sort of the greatest guy. He's odd. He had a lot of odd insights into things, and I guess I did, too. It was two odd insights meeting."

Years later, when Byrne turned those odd insights into a marketable commodity, Kehoe was taken aback. Kehoe couldn't understand how an audience could make such a big deal out of what, to him, were everyday jokes and attitudes. The difference between Byrne and Kehoe was that David realized that, with their shared cracked perspective, they were onto something.

"David was really lousy at the guitar," alleged Melissa Kearney, who grew up to become an opera singer. "At the time, he could only play one/four/five/one chords really loud, with a lot of static. It didn't surprise me that David became successful, but it did surprise me that he became a musician."

When Byrne realized that Melissa was a good singer, he suggested she join Bizadi. Melissa, young and eager, agreed immediately. Her first show with the Byrne-Kehoe duo was at Baltimore's Fells Point Art Gallery. She had never re-hearsed with Bizadi, but Byrne assured her that would be no problem—he'd provide fake books and they'd sight-read while they performed. The performance began smoothly.

"Everything was going like a nice little jazz scene,"

Melissa recalled. "David got frustrated because everything was going so straight. So he took our fake books and threw them away. Then we had no music to read, so we all had to improvise. It became sort of a happening, a John Cage kind of sound.

"I started to sing 'Stormy Weather'—'I can't go on, everything I had is gone'—and David poured a bucket of water on my head. I was holding a 120-watt microphone! I threw the microphone and sparks started coming out of it.

"But it was sort of funny."

Byrne and Kehoe had to leave a halfway decent apartment when the landlord took out all the plumbing. They moved into a loft across the street from a fish market. In the summer the place smelled like fish. Still, friends stayed over all the time.

"[Byrne] had this flat affect all the time," Melissa claimed. "If you can imagine the *opposite* of someone being hysterical, it was David. Yet he was very emotional inside. Although he came on like he didn't care about anything, I think he thought very deeply about life."

Melissa recalled the one time she saw Byrne lose control. "Once I went to visit Mark and David, and, as I got close, I saw his girlfriend Joan Lobell come running out of the house. Then I saw David come running out of the house screaming. It was funny when David screamed. It was like his singing voice, sort of a flat-pitched scream. But he was really pissed. Joan thought he hadn't been paying enough attention to her, so in revenge she unplugged his guitar from his amplifier. He really went berserk."

But, she went on, "David was a walking art form. Somehow everybody could hook into it and know what he was talking about. There was sort of a sense of life that we all had then."

As for real life, Byrne and Kehoe's financial futures were

dirt low and sinking. Baltimore was a tough, working-class city, block upon block of row houses that had changed very little since the Great Depression. At that time a law had been enacted that allowed Baltimore homeowners to convert their living rooms into businesses; as a result, many city neighborhoods were still dotted with home-grown bars and beauty parlors. Without jobs or money, Byrne and Kehoe rode around in cars for recreation.

The Fells Point section where Kehoe and Byrne lived was something of a haven for impoverished artists. John Waters, the underground filmmaker famed for *Pink Flamingos*, was star of the scene. Byrne and Kehoe got to know Waters and his circle of bizarre friends.

Waters delighted in the most tasteless and tacky aspects of American culture. He wore boxy suits and slicked his hair straight back, much as David Byrne someday would. Waters's humor was a sort of earlier, creepier version of David Letterman's: professing wide-eyed interest while snickering up his sleeve. Waters claimed to love the *National Enquirer* and its lunatic sister the *Weekly World News*. Years later, Byrne would use those publications as inspirations for his own screenplay, *True Stories*.

Although David grew friendly with Waters, he and Kehoe were more likely to hang out with Edith the Egg Lady, a Fells Point celebrity notable for her girth (she weighed about three hundred pounds). "We used to drive her around." The colorful scene had its down side, however.

"Most of those John Waters people couldn't act and didn't act," said Kevin Kearney. "They just sort of lived a very strange life-style. An awful lot of people in Fells Point —sculptors, painters—got caught up in being dead ends. As you can see, David didn't."

In autumn 1972, Naomi left Baltimore to go to RISD. Kehoe began spending more time in Providence, where he got a job playing accordion on weekends at Joe's, a sandwich shop that was an RISD hangout. Byrne joined some friends on a trip to California.

"The sandwich shop was owned by a nice, friendly, wild guy named Dewey," Kehoe explained. "He was about three hundred and fifty pounds, with hair down to here. He paid me fifty dollars to play accordion, which was like a million dollars to me."

It was the sort of idyllic life another man would have stuck to. But, as his railing walking and cigar butt smoking showed, Kehoe could not resist a dare. When Dewey decided to drive out to California, he challenged Kehoe to hitchhike there and meet him in ten days; his reward would be a trip back in Dewey's Mercedes. Kehoe, with twenty dollars in his pocket, left the next day. He made it to California but passed up his reward to stay with David at the Sausalito home of the family of a RISD student they knew.

"The mother was weird," Kehoe maintained. "She kept saying, 'It's the first cantilevered house in Sausalito!' It was a weird house. They were obsessed by saying, 'There are no corners here. Everything is a rhombus.' They had a black maid named America. She kicked us out because we were so dirty."

For shelter David bought a two-tone 1956 DeSoto with a bullet hole in the windshield. He and Kehoe lived in it for two weeks, flipping coins to see who got to avoid sleeping in front with the steering wheel. To raise money for their trip home, the duo began playing on street corners in San Francisco and Berkeley. They were soon joined by a saxophonist and became, Kehoe recalls, an avant-garde jazz band for about a week and a half. "We got a couple of gigs at this cafe in Berkeley. It was just, 'Immerse yourself and play what you feel.' "

Christmas was coming, and David's DeSoto had passed

on to the boneyard. At least in California the boys might have expected to be warm. But no: "It snowed for the first time in thirty-five years," Kehoe sighed. So Byrne and Kehoe thumbed home, arriving in Baltimore on Christmas Eve. About a month later, Kehoe moved up to Providence to be with Naomi. Deciding that Providence was in every way a healthier environment than Baltimore, he went back south and soon convinced Byrne to join him.

Back in Rhode Island, Byrne, Kehoe, and Naomi moved into a big house on Brown Street on Providence's East Side, a neighborhood where old New England wealth clung to little islands amid a rising tide of migrant students, artists, and layabouts. The campuses of Brown University and RISD overlapped there, on the border between the blue-bloods and the youngbloods.

"David and Mark and a whole bunch of people were living in this crazy place," recalled Rudy Cheeks, who met Byrne in Providence. "I visited there a lot. It was a big, huge house. I guess it really should have been condemned. Naomi was living there, too, and a woman named Elisca Jeansonne. Elisca was a Cajun from New Orleans. She used to make clothes with animal tails on them. Everybody in the house was wild. David had this cheap electric guitar up in his room. His room was an incredible mess."

Cheeks had a band called the Motels (not to be confused with the Martha Davis–led band of the same name), a gonzo ensemble that combined rock, comedy, and theater. Drummer David Hansen's patterns were doubled exactly by Dan Gosch on a tiny toy drum kit. Charles Rocket (who later replaced Bill Murray on *Saturday Night Live*) played accordion. Three female singers, the Tantalizing Tampoons, parodied the Ikettes. Years later, Byrne would say that the Motels were the funniest thing he had ever seen.

The group was an offshoot of a late-sixties RISD comedy/

music/art scene whose central figure, comedian/musician Martin Mull, had already left Providence for Hollywood when Byrne and Kehoe arrived.

"As soon as David got here," Cheeks said, "he gravitated to what was obviously the weirdest stuff going on—which was us. He was a good guy; he was on the right wavelength."

Byrne made an impression on the "in" crowd right off. He and Kehoe came to a Motels gig at RISD and asked if Bizadi could perform at intermission. The Motels agreed.

"David played violin with a little bird attached to the end of the bow," Dan Gosch recalled. "Mark played accordion. They did 'Pennies from Heaven,' and during an instrumental interlude David shaved his beard off. There were no aisles or anything, the floor was completely filled with people. Someone gave him a can of beer from the first row, and he sort of soaked his beard down and shaved it, bleeding."

As Cheeks remembered it, "David shaved his beard to the rhythm of the song, Mark played the accordion and danced around. Naomi passed out photocopies of a picture of Vladimir Lenin signed, *Sincerely Yours, Walter Kaputska.*"

"[Byrne] cut himself to ribbons," said Motel Jeff Shore. "It was a real dada experience. Naomi had an easel with Russian words written on shirt cardboards on it. She kept exposing new Russian words while Mark played the accordion and David cut himself to pieces. David had on a hat with a woman's high-heeled shoe and electric lights on it. I remember rivulets of blood pouring down his neck as people groaned in sympathy."

This, Byrne's only known instance of incorporating sadomasochism into a performance, was typically prescient: In a few years, bloodletting would become a favored stage business among certain flamboyant punk rockers.

"It was really quite an act," Dan Gosch commented. "Interesting first impression."

Byrne, Kehoe, and Naomi were gathered to the bosom of

the Motels' crowd, who accepted wild clothes and oddball humor as a commendable response to the twilight of the Age of Aquarius.

"This was the early seventies," Kehoe explained. "It was a weird time culturally. The sixties were over and we wanted to go on to something different. That's why we did things like wear leopard-skin pants. Girls in stockings and high heels just seemed so radical. It seems ridiculous now, but it was us saying 'pooooh' to this whole established sixties against-the-culture thing, which had become so dead and silly.

"We started making all our own clothes because normal clothes were not good enough for us. I was always making sure I had the pointiest shoes that I could find, with Cuban heels, and silk stockings and sunglasses. I guess it was shocking to people."

Meanwhile, David had bleached his hair, an act that suggests the influence of the prevailing rock/pop glitter scene epitomized by David Bowie, a.k.a. Ziggy Stardust, but which probably had more to do with the influence of Naomi, who'd recently streaked her own dark tresses. Soon after that, Naomi recalled, she returned from a trip to find David with light orange hair. "I said 'David! What did you use?' He said, 'Clorox.' "

"David wasn't at RISD very long," said Rudy Cheeks. "He was part of the campus scene and part of the art scene —especially the underground weirdo art scene—but he wasn't a real RISD guy. I was under the impression that he was totally a conceptual artist. I never saw any paintings. The only thing I ever saw were his questionnaires.

"We'd have parties and David would invariably show up with questionnaires that he'd pass out. They were usually about outer space: 'Do you believe there's life on other planets?' He seemed to have a real interest in aliens."

"[I was] fascinated by conceptual art," Byrne himself

admitted. "In particular, there was some that just used language. They'd just write a statement on the wall, and others would put out little pamphlets. There was a group called Art and Language that just talked all the time in print. And I thought that was pretty much the ultimate in refining and eliminating all the superfluous stuff in art and being left with nothing but the idea."

One classmate remembered Byrne tape recording people saying, "Things that were different," an early harbinger of Byrne's own collectivist approach to narrative on his 1985 solo LP, *Music from the Knee Plays*. Another said Byrne made a series of maps of the New Jersey Turnpike at different scales.

None of this paid the rent. Luckily, David found work in a New York System wiener joint, one of a string of diners ubiquitous in Rhode Island but unknown elsewhere, including New York.

"David worked nights," Rudy Cheeks explained. "He'd be working the grill and he used to tell me stories about fights breaking out. It was on Smith Hill, a pretty tough place in a pretty rough neighborhood. He told me that during a fight somebody dropped a pot of mustard on another guy's head. He just watched it, amazed. He was a pretty good grill man and wanted to move up, but I thought that (a) he wasn't that good and (b) the main problem was that his arms were kind of hairy. When he lined wieners up on his arms, people might have been put off. I felt he was doomed to failure as a grill man, which was music's gain."

By now Byrne had another old car, this one notable for a rubber gorilla stuck on the front hood and cutouts of the states on the trunk. Naomi and Kehoe usually drove the car and put gas in it, however; from all accounts, driving was not one of David's major talents. When the car broke down on an out-of-town trip, David decided to leave it by the roadside. But before he left, Rudy Cheeks remembers, "He got a piece of cardboard and a crayon and wrote in big letters, THIS CAR IS BROKEN, and put it on the car. That's the way he talked. It's like, 'The name of this band is Talking Heads.' That's David."

David had begun writing songs. Byrne said that "Psycho Killer" was the first song he ever wrote and that he was trying to combine Alice Cooper with Randy Newman. The phrase was already a favorite expression among Byrne's RISD compatriots.

"Barbara Conway, one of the Tampoons, used to use that all the time," says Rudy Cheeks. She used to call people 'psycho killers.' 'That guy's just a psycho killer!' We shortened it to 'PK' after a while. We called people PK's." (Cruel irony. In 1985, Barbara Conway was murdered, apparently by a real lunatic, in her Rhode Island home. She left a husband and two small children.)

"I remember when David was writing the song," Naomi said. "We were sitting in his room on Brown Street. He had this notebook on his bed and he was reading us the words. We were all laughing because of the French stuff. David laughed, too."

David got help with his composition from a couple of RISD students much straighter than he: Chris Frantz and Tina Weymouth.

"David said, 'I've got an idea for a song,' " Chris recalled five years later. "I think he had the words for the first verse. We worked on the middle part, the bridge, the French part."

Tina Weymouth explained, "The part about 'I hate people when they aren't polite,' the vainness, was because we didn't want to talk about the obvious things dwelt on with psycho killers."

The use of *fa fa fa fa*, a take-off on Otis Redding, was Byrne's idea; he wanted to have as many clichés in the song as possible, according to Tina. "It was going to be a pop song that everybody could relate to. It was going to have a conventional rock structure."

Tina's mother was French, and as a child she had spent lots of time in France. She brought that perspective to the new song:

"We put in *yeah yeahs* and *ooh ooh babys*. Those were French clichés. They called rock & roll 'ya-ya music.' When rock & roll first hit France in 1960, they also called it 'new wave.' At first they did French versions of American songs by people like Elvis Presley and Buddy Holly. Then they started writing their own songs. I was familiar with that because I'm half French. That's why the French part got put into 'Psycho Killer.' "

Years later, Byrne would offer another explanation: "It seemed a natural delusion that a psychotic killer would imagine himself as very refined and use a foreign language to talk to himself."

The success of "Psycho Killer" among Byrne's peers set the whole gang to work writing songs. Kehoe came up with some that never made it onto record. A RISD pal named Wayne Zieve produced "Artists Only," the lyrics of which would appear on the second Talking Heads album, *More Songs about Buildings and Food*.

Byrne was clearly onto something. He recruited Chris Frantz and some other campus musicians to form the Artistics. Chris and Tina, who would later marry, were not yet boyfriend and girlfriend. They were serious painting students from upscale backgrounds. His father was a general and an attorney; hers was an admiral. But rock & roll was, for the baby boomers, a potent class leveler. Shared ambition, too, can initiate strange alliances. Chris and David were both smart guys, both self-considered artists, and both loved pop music.

"Chris was always into music a lot," recalled David

Hansen, one of the Motels. "Chris and Tina were both painters, but Chris talked about music more than he talked about painting."

"Chris Frantz took a year off after high school and was in a band for that year, before he went to college," Kehoe revealed. "He played at the Electric Circus on St. Mark's Place when it was at the end of its hot-spot era. I guess he always saw himself as a professional drummer."

How real a band the Artistics were, however, is debated in Providence to this day.

Rudy Cheeks: "They were a garage band. They had a couple of gigs at the RISD Tap Room. It wasn't really like a band."

Dan Gosch: "I saw them whenever I could. I read somewhere that they only played, like, eight times. That may be. They did 'Psycho Killer,' they did 'Warning Sign.' They did a terrific version of '1, 2, 3 Red Light.' I always thought that they should include that on an album. It was very Talking Headsy. I think they did '96 Tears.' "

Naomi: "They used to play up in the Tap Room. They were great."

David Hansen: "It was a terrible band."

Perhaps recalling Bizadi's acceptance at the Fells Point Art Gallery, Byrne and Kehoe decided it would be a great idea for David's new band to play at an exhibit at RISD's Woods-Gerry Gallery. In fact, they could even improve on the Fells Point precedent; this time the art on display would be the work of Kehoe, Byrne, and Naomi. There was only one problem: Of the three of them, only Naomi was enrolled at RISD. Kehoe and Byrne hung around campus, enjoyed student perks like fifty-cent movies, but generally looked down their noses at the whole college scene. Still, they were pragmatists, and if they could use college facilities for their own ends, great. If they could poke a little fun at academia at the same time, all the better. Along with the art display, Byrne and Kehoe planned to display Mark and Naomi in gorilla costumes singing "My Baby Must Be a Magician" (an old Marvelettes tune) while the Artistics provided musical accompaniment.

So Byrne and Kehoe drove to Boston, an hour from RISD, to gather material for their soiree. They spent all their money renting gorilla suits, buying liquor—it would be radical to serve martinis instead of the traditional wine—and stocking up on magazines. One of David's notions was to put on display an easy chair alongside a table covered with that month's magazines—all sorts, including porno.

"And," Kehoe said, "David, Naomi, and I took billions of Polaroids. Each of us had a Polaroid camera and it was always *click, click, click*. Some of the Polaroids were nudes, some were of people dressed up as the opposite sex."

Kehoe left for work while the show was being hung and was upset to come back and find that Byrne had taken over a room for his own sheets of typed paper, consigning Kehoe's paintings and photographs to a less significant spot.

Sometimes ambition is the undoing of even the greatest minds. Not content with an audience of students and pals, the Brown Street Three had put up signs all over Providence inviting the public to their exhibit. The signs promised cocktails, too.

"Lunatics from all over the world were showing up for this show," Rudy Cheeks said. "If you were an artist of dubious sanity, it was the place to be. Somehow people from RISD got word of what was going on. At the last minute, they canceled the show. When I got there, I was told that Mark and David said for everybody to come over to the house on Brown Street. They were bringing all the liquor over there. But Mark and David and Wayne Zieve had to go to Massachusetts to return a gorilla suit or something."

Indeed, since the gorilla suits were no longer *de rigeur*, Byrne and company figured to save a day's rental by returning them to Boston. This was during the 1974 gas crisis, however, and in Boston the trio found themselves stuck without fuel. They finally decided to visit Zieve's uncle Don, who lived in a nearby suburb.

"At the time we all wore weird clothes," Kehoe explained. "Leather pants, leopard skin, and fake fur jackets. We always had black or red thumbnails and sort of rooster-chopped haircuts. Uncle Don and his wife were not very happy. It was an ultra-uptight atmosphere, but it was obvious they were looking at us like, 'Well, Wayne *is* our nephew.'

"He said, 'Well, you guys must be hungry.'

" 'Yes, we are, Uncle Don.'

" 'Well, I'll tell the wife.'

"They brought us a platter of toast. They cut it into points. I think there was butter."

Back in Providence the booze and freeloaders and porno magazines had all come together at Brown Street to ignite a shindig of mythical proportions. At Uncle Don's, Kehoe recalled, "We were allowed to sleep on chairs in the den. In the morning we got gas and went back. We missed the party."

In spring 1974, the Artistics disintegrated as RISD graduation lured the members toward different careers. Byrne had built up a head of rock & roll steam, only to find his sidemen turning into adults and grad students. It must have seemed a gift from the gods when the Motels broke up at the same time, and some of them started putting together a new group. All they needed was a guitar player.

"We were going to start a more mainstream band," Jeff Shore said. "A David Bowie and the Spiders from Mars type of thing with Charlie Rocket being the David Bowie type.

We thought we needed a flashy Mick Ronson type of guitarist. We auditioned about ten guitarists and nobody worked out. So Charlie said, 'My friend David Byrne plays guitar. He's going to come by and audition.'

"I remember David walked in the door wearing a Boston Red Sox cap. He looked really lost, kind of nervous, and shy to the extreme. We talked for a few minutes and then he started playing. We played all these songs he had just written: 'Psycho Killer,' 'The Girls Want to Be with the Girls.' "

Charles Rocket recalled that Byrne also had a song called "Sick Boy"—"it went, 'Sick boy, I don't feel well' "—presumably another attempt by Byrne to rework the material of "Psycho Killer." Considering the impact "Psycho Killer" eventually had on David's public image, it's probably fortunate that "Sick Boy" died.

"He played all these songs for us," Jeff Shore said. "And then we started saying, 'Okay, now let's do some of our songs.' But at that point, he could barely play the guitar. He could play some rhythm chords, but forget about lead-guitar abilities. We wanted a flashy guitarist, and he just couldn't cut it. I remember a piercing look from David Byrne as he left, a kind of superior look like, 'You don't know what you're missing.' "

Soon after that, Byrne left Providence for New York City.

2

"The best thing about art school," Tina Weymouth has said, "is that you might just happen to run into people with ideas similar to your own. That's what Roxy Music was, and that's pretty much what happened with us, too."

Everyone agrees that Martina Weymouth was a very tough woman, a woman who knew what she wanted and got it. Some people hated her for that and others loved her for it.

Because Tina's father was an admiral, she grew up moving from place to place. Her mother was French, a doctor's daughter from a society family. Tina is the third of eight siblings; she has five sisters and two brothers. They spent summer vacations at a house in Brittany; Tina spoke French quite well.

"Believe it or not," Tina said, "I'm a very shy person. But as long as I don't act shy in front of you, you don't know. That's something I learned very young, when I was six. Because I moved around every year, I had to make friends. So I learned, 'Pretend you're not shy and no one will know the difference.'

"It's like applying for a job. You know you won't get the job unless you've had experience, but you can't get the experience unless you get the job. So what you do is, you lie. Because you know that on the first day, since every office has its own method of doing things, they're going to tell you letter by letter how to work every machine. Even though you've already said in your application that you know how to operate them, they're going to make you go over the whole thing. So you learn right then and there—and then you know how."

That's a remarkable story, as it reveals both a degree of guile (misrepresenting one's past to get ahead is treated as sensible) and impressive self-assurance (Tina assumes she will be able to pick up specialized skills by quick observation).

In high school, Tina became entranced by rock & roll: "I was living in California. I would try to sneak into the Whisky à Go-Go because that was the one place you could get in if you were underage. I'd see Paul Revere and the Raiders jumping in the pool at Marineland, and I always felt they had such extraordinarily exciting lives. But it was always something I was seeing on the TV screen, or through the car window, just passing by.

"I'd listen to the radio, trying to get that setting of excitement. The radio was playing really good songs. When I was sixteen, one of the big hits was 'Love Is All Around' by the Troggs, and Cream had 'Sunshine of Your Love.' Stuff like that created an atmosphere of excitement that you believed was incredibly intense. You thought a lot of people were having more fun than you were. I played guitar, I did drawings and paintings, but I didn't know what I wanted to be. I was completely confused. I had no idea."

Even a stint as captain of the cheerleading squad failed to make Tina feel she belonged.

"Materialism had a lot to do with it," she said. "The kids I went to high school with in California had a lot of toys: cars, telephones in their rooms, TV sets. They bought a lot of clothes at the shopping mall every Saturday, and radios and records and drugs. It seemed like they were really in trouble. Their parents gave them all of this, and yet something was missing."

As a child in Washington, D.C., Tina had studied art at the Corçoran School of Art—Mark Rothko, she said, was one of her teachers—but when it was time for college she first tried Barnard and an academic program.

"I was doing a double major in French literature and art history," Tina said. "It was the time when everything was falling apart. It was 1970 and life didn't mean anything anymore. People were getting killed at Kent State. Nobody wanted to have grades anymore. Girls and boys didn't want to have separate dorms anymore. Things were changing and people were losing interest in academics. I got real disillusioned, and I dropped out of college and got a job. Then I thought, 'Now I know why you go to college. You go to college to avoid this!' So then I applied to RISD."

At RISD Tina shared a studio with Kentucky blueblood Chris Frantz, whose father was just as military as hers and who was, Tina thought, a real Southern gentleman. Chris was seriously working at being an artist. He did big paintings in acrylics.

"Adolescents who fancy themselves artistic people," Chris said, explaining his creative impulse, "read about people like Gauguin and think, 'Oh, that's what I'm going to be like. Because I feel the same things. I'm an outsider, too.' "

But devoted as Chris was to painting, he couldn't get the rock & roll bug out of his system. The Artistics had reactivated his old instincts, and though he wasn't ready to join David Byrne in New York immediately after graduation, neither was he writing off future collaborations. "I always liked the colorful people who lived in Providence," Chris said. "There are a lot of real eccentrics there, and if you live there long enough you turn into one."

Contemplating his future, Chris decided to visit a fortune

teller. "He asked her if he should be a drummer or a painter," recalled Jamie Dalglish, a RISD friend. "She looked at his hands and said, 'You should be a drummer, you'll have great success.' "

It's been widely assumed, both by those who view Talking Heads as a cynically executed project and by those who see it as an idealistic endeavor, that when David Byrne left RISD for New York in May 1974 the Talking Heads were ready to roll. In fact, his early months in New York seem to have been Byrne's period of greatest indecision.

His faithful sidekicks, Kehoe and Naomi, were in love. They wanted no one but each other. They'd moved out of the house on Brown Street to an apartment on Federal Hill so that they could be alone.

Alone—in other words, without David. Chris and Tina were not yet major forces in Byrne's life. But if David had hoped that he and Chris could build a new, more serious Artistics in Manhattan, that dream was deferred by the new graduate's reluctance to move too quickly.

One evening Byrne appeared at Leo's, the Providence restaurant/hangout where Naomi waitressed. He studied a matchbook ad for computer dating and said—sincerely, Naomi thought—that he should fill out and send in the lonely hearts come-on. After all, everyone else had somebody.

The Artistics had fizzled. Nobody took them seriously and anyway, they weren't that good. The Motels, who *were* good, had spurned Byrne. A lot of people now say that Byrne went to New York to execute a master plan. But looking objectively at his fortunes in early 1974, it seems more likely that he was getting out of a Providence scene in which he no longer felt at home.

Since none of his other friends was in any hurry to emigrate, Byrne hooked up with Jamie Dalglish, who had worked in a video studio in Providence, where Byrne would come in with different ideas for shows.

"He was a wild and crazy guy," Dalglish said. "He used to dress up in funny outfits. He wanted to teach an art history class about UFOs. The teacher didn't go for that."

Dalglish found a big loft on the ground level at Bond Street just off the Bowery. It was a rotten neighborhood, but it was a great apartment. While Chris and Tina and other RISD friends were attending graduation ceremonies, Byrne and Dalglish were renovating in New York City.

Byrne and Dalglish slaved over renovating the rundown loft. They pulled the nails out of the floor one by one, sanded, and painted. At the end of all their labors, Dalglish had a place that was nice by any criterion and palatial by Bowery standards.

Byrne had no job, but Dalglish let him stay at his new place. At first Dalglish wasn't sure what to make of his new roommate.

"I came home one day and found David under a huge radiator," Dalglish said. "He was holding the radiator as if it were squashing him, as if someone had thrown it out the window and it landed on him. He acted like I wasn't in the room.

"He was always doing things like that. I couldn't tell if he was doing a show for me or just experiencing a funny situation. It was like body art. Then I began to pick up on his humor a little more. It was eking out.

"Minimalism was in, as were big-scale works backed by millions of dollars. So David did a piece called 'Number of Consecutive Days without Error,' with three slots in which you put numbers. You'd come home from work at the end of the day and keep tabs on your errors. It was pretty funny."

Byrne was also writing the songs he'd later sing at CBGB, though he didn't have a band.

Into this beatnik Eden came a woman. Andrea Kovacs
had been at RISD when Byrne arrived from Baltimore but
had left Providence for grad school at Yale before David got
in with the Motels crowd. Andrea, a statuesque femme
fatale with a sharp disposition, remembered Byrne as a campus oddball behind whose back she laughed. But she was
friends with Dalglish, whose Bond Street loft was to become, in Andrea's words, "the Ellis Island of the Providence
migration to New York."

Andrea walked into Dalglish's place one summer day in
1974 and saw, in the middle of the room, a hollowed-out
redwood log. Curled up inside the log, like a fetus in utero,
was David Byrne.

"At RISD," Andrea recalled, "I had been repelled by
David—he looked then like a crazed lumberjack who'd just
come out of the woods after rolling a few too many logs. But
now I was quite taken by this man. His beard was gone, and
he had tremendous physical appeal to me. He looked very
strong. His head, neck, and chest were strong and tapered
to a point like a cornucopia. He had a thick black head of
hair. He looked like a Taurean, a bull."

There was a romantic buzz between Andrea and Dalglish,
who was suggesting she move into the Bond Street haven.
Byrne might well have supposed that he was about to become third wheel again. But here the pattern of the previous
triads took an unexpected twist. This time, the woman came
on to David instead of to his friend.

"It was very late, a couple of nights later," Andrea said.
"Jamie had gone to bed. David and I were listening to Lou
Reed's 'Sister Ray.' I passed David a cryptic little message
—a note about what I felt about him. He responded immediately. It was like spontaneous ignition. We were together from that moment on."

This sudden romance may have been a burst of white

light for the lonesome Byrne, but it was a shot in the chops to Dalglish. He now had two lovebirds nesting in his place, too wrapped up in each other to think about earthly matters like rent.

"David and I were having a tremendously good time together," Andrea explained. "We slept in Jamie's kitchen on a mattress. We just moved in without any consideration of Jamie's feelings. It was an uncontrollable thing."

Byrne and Andrea passed the summer days sitting on the front stoop, drinking wine and speaking in tongues loosed by youth, love, and ambition. They'd wander across the street to CBGB, a new Bowery rock club, where they'd play pool and the jukebox. "96 Tears" was David's favorite and Andrea came to think of it as their song.

Wrapped up in each other though they were, Andrea felt the distance between her heritage, her upbringing, and Byrne's.

"I like spewing up emotions and dealing with them," she explained. "David was much more cerebral, analytical. At times it was difficult for us. I was groping with my own problems, but I was still in school and had the luxury of time. David was already in New York, trying to survive.

"He was always analyzing life's systems, wondering if they were real or not. He was an agnostic, not just about God but toward what people accept as truths about life. He didn't believe in some of the realities of the world. It was very difficult for David to believe in love. 'Is it hype or is it real?': He was full of questions about it. He wanted love. He was almost in love with the *concept* of being in love. He was the most romantic man I ever knew. He told me that he had never been in love in his life, that he had never experienced it. David doesn't believe in anything until he tests it out for himself. He was very committed to finding the experience of love—and he was frightened of it."

Byrne often told Andrea that he was afraid of getting in over his head. Andrea encouraged him to let go.

Andrea's parents, in the grand tradition, disapproved of David. One summer day she agreed to bring her new boyfriend to a family outing in Babylon, a Long Island beach community. The dark-haired, pale-skinned, black-garbed couple stood out among the blond, suntanned beach crowd. But they gave it a good try.

Byrne and Andrea went sailing and sunbathing on her uncle's boat. A snapshot from that afternoon shows Byrne looking calm, healthy, and startlingly handsome. Back on shore, though, the relatives started whispering.

"I felt there was a scathing review taking place," Andrea said. "I had to get away. David and I left and walked down a serpentine road with bushes everywhere and very bright sun. I was very tense. I was walking ahead of him. Suddenly he embraced me from behind. He held me and said, 'What's the matter?' I explained that I felt awkward. That I felt we were misfits there. At that moment I think he understood that I was very alone, and that he could open up to me. He started to talk about love, about our relationship. Then he said, 'I've gone in over my head.'

"That was the turning point in our relationship. It was suddenly like we were the only two people in a jungle."

Andrea's mother and her stepfather, a college professor, drove the young lovers back to the city—and took the occasion to berate their daughter's boyfriend.

"My stepfather was hostile," Andrea said. "We were captives in the back of the car. He said to David, 'You'll never amount to anything if you don't get your college education! You're just going to be a nobody your whole life!' He went on and on like this. It was just unbelievable. I sat there thinking, 'Why is this happening?' "

Andrea had a nasty streak of her own. When Dalglish's

girlfriend Susan moved into the Bond Street loft, Andrea launched a reign of terror against the woman she saw as an intruder in her domain—this in spite of the fact that it was Dalglish's place and that Byrne and Andrea were the real outsiders.

"David and I had a sense of humor that hermetically sealed us," Andrea recalled. "David is a very humorous guy. Much of our time was spent almost in judgment of the people and things around us. It was us against the world. We built a wall around ourselves. There was a tremendous symbiotic support system there for a while."

As the summer passed, Byrne confessed to Andrea that he was at a standstill about what to do with his future. He had a grand ambition: to make his life into a work of conceptual art, to design a persona and then animate it. He wanted to create an artificial personality. What would make it art would be not just the creation, but that no one would *know* that the created David Byrne wasn't real.

But what form should this created persona take? That had Byrne stumped.

Finally he hit on the answer: Byrne would become a *systems analyst.* He explained to Andrea that he would devote his entire life to computer programming. He would call it a life system; it would be an art project. And he would do so anonymously.

"It was obscure conceptualism," Andrea said with notable restraint. "I encouraged him not to do it. I said there was more to life, and anyway, it would be a shame not to let people *know* about his art."

In the days that followed, Byrne became more depressed about his future. He would spend hours lying on his mattress, on his belly, with his arms straight at his sides. Nobody could rouse him.

"He was having a lot of problems, I think," Andrea said. "He was in New York and wanted to make it big and did not know how. He couldn't focus his energy. The environment was controlling him. He was not ready to control his environment. He was like a collapsed star."

With summer ending, Andrea had to think about getting back up to Yale. But she couldn't very well leave her boyfriend prostrate and morose. Byrne later answered an ad for a movie usher; he got the job.

Andrea went back to school in New Haven. Byrne would come up on the bus on weekends. He played her records by Brian Eno, the British art-rock minimalist. She scanned his body with a Polaroid camera and made montages of the photos.

Andrea was getting back into campus life. At Yale she was a hotshot, somewhat wild artist in an intellectual community. Byrne often showed up for his visits in weird clothes. Once he arrived wearing a big suit, an oversize ensemble that struck Andrea as an attempt to parody people like computer programmers. She began to feel a little embarrassed by her oddball movie usher boyfriend with his big suits and started dating another campus heavy, a Hungarian student.

"I think David was going through such a bad period," she said. "He held on to me like a lifeline. I knew his ideas and his dreams. He had opened up to me. I was an artist, I was very popular at school; in a way I represented what he wanted for his life.

"One day David showed up in a grotesque white plastic raincoat. He was pale. Something about the way he was dressed revolted me. It was his weakness, his groping showing. I was very cruel. I had no compassion for him. I told him, 'Get out. Just go home.' Why was I doing this? I didn't explain. He started to grab for some books, some things he'd left there. I said, 'Get your books and get out.' It was very cold. I put down an iron curtain.

"Maybe I'm just trying to justify it, but I hope somehow

what went on between us forced him to do what he had to do to become a creator. Sometimes an anger grounds you and pushes you forward."

Providence enjoyed a late summer in 1974. When the kids came back to RISD the weather was still beautiful, and all the trees were green. Chris Frantz had just received his college degree and told Mary Clarke, a backup singer with the Motels, that he was going to go to New York to join a band with David. Although she was no great fan of the Artistics, Mary said she thought Chris and David might be on to something.

Jeff Turtletaub, another RISD immigrant to New York, thought it interesting for the same reason: "People with any kind of bohemian sensibilities were becoming artists. Other people went into more legitimate professions. But the idea of being in a *band* was pretty open. Very few people of mature ambition were taking that route. It was amazing no one thought of it sooner. There were no obstacles."

Byrne had already been spending much of his time at CBGB, the rock club across the street from Dalglish's loft. He watched the early gigs of Mink DeVille, Debbie Harry's Stilettoes and Blondie, the Ramones, and the Patti Smith Group.

CBGB had been open less than a year, but its policy of employing rock bands performing original compositions gave it a significance to local scenemakers, including the music press. Max's Kansas City was a better-known club, but that made it tougher to break into. By late 1974, Max's was booking more mainstream, flashy young performers like Bruce Springsteen, Hall and Oates, and Bob Marley's Wailers. CBGB was number two; they were more inclined to hire bands still raw and struggling to pull their music together.

"Even before David moved to New York," Turtletaub

said, "he told me about CBGB: 'There's this place we could play.' We used to go down there and see Television, Patti Smith, the Ramones. I'm sure that helped shape the direction of Talking Heads. Ultimately, you can call David a musician or a punk rocker, but I think that's way off the mark. David was a very astute businessman. He was very smart, very shrewd. He approached it in a businesslike way.

"What David saw was a gap in the market. You might say he anticipated yuppies. He anticipated the whole baby-boom generation growing up. When he went down there, there was glitter rock and stuff, but that music appealed only to people of a certain age. It was obvious these people were getting older and were ready for something new and different."

One night, Turtletaub and Byrne went over to Tina's brother's house on Long Island. David said, "We've decided Tina's going to join the band. She's going to play bass. In fact, there's her bass."

"I remember seeing her with her brand-new bass," Turtletaub said, "and thinking, 'What a brilliant move!' Chris and Tina were the *cleanest* people around. The whole image was just so perfect. What David got from Chris and Tina was a kind of *blondness* that other people didn't have. They had a definite look and a style and a kind of softening around the edges that made the whole thing much more palatable. Chris and Tina were like America's darlings. David could get up there and act like a chicken with his head cut off, but Tina looked fine, so that made it okay. And it made it more interesting, 'cause they were something he could play off. The contrast made you notice."

Contrast, of course, has long since become part of Byrne's performing stock in trade, from the layered polyrhythms of *Remain in Light* to the ever-expanding series of visual and musical buildups and releases that galvanize *Stop Making*

Sense. Much of Byrne's inspiration for his *Music from the Knee Plays* album, he has admitted, stemmed from a desire to "combine opposites . . . after a while I saw I could believe in something and also its opposite."

But Byrne also appreciated this couple who believed in him and whose personalities suggested relative stability, along with a strong sense of artistic purpose.

"Before Chris and Tina," Turtletaub explained, "David was with Mark Kehoe and Naomi. Those days were fun, but crazy. Chris and Tina came from money. David had been pretty poor. He'd been doing horrible jobs. Chris and Tina enveloped him in a kind of bourgeois situation. David's old friends were like him, kind of on the edge. Chris and Tina always seemed to know what was going on. Culturally and socially they were from very strong backgrounds. By aligning himself with them, David gave himself a certain kind of cushion."

Chris and Tina gained at least as much from hitching onto Byrne's creativity as David gained from their clear-headed career-mindedness. "They supported David," Kehoe said. "He moved in with them when they got their loft on Christie Street. They knew David was going somewhere."

Kehoe, still living in Providence with Naomi, may have been hurt to see Byrne shift allegiances. But, he recalls, he still rejected overtures from Tina to play keyboards with the new band. "I thought it was boring," he remembers ruefully. "My head turned into a big lollipop: *sucker.*"

Jamie Dalglish's apartment was the center for stepped-up immigrant activity. Mary Clarke moved down from Providence, as did Wayne Zieve. With Andrea gone, Susan had no rival for the position of hostess. Soon she and Jamie announced their engagement.

Chris and Tina found a loft nearby on Christie Street. David spent most of his time there. Unfortunately, that loft had no bath or shower, so Byrne, Chris, and Tina would all come to Dalglish's to bathe. There was a lot of talk about the new band at Dalglish's—particularly about the decision to include Tina as the bass player. "Some were jealous," said Mary Clarke, "some thought it was a good idea, some thought it was a dumb idea. It caused an uproar."

Wayne Zieve needed a place to stay, and Dalglish's floor space was already claimed. He moved into the Christie Street loft, where he got to watch the new trio's first rehearsals, cowrite a song, and name the band.

"Talking Heads" was a term coined in a *TV Guide* article to describe TV programs—talk shows and news reports—in which the visuals were limited to face shots.

"We had written down about a hundred names to choose from," Zieve recalled. "Talking Heads just came from my impression of the band. David didn't really sing that much. He would yell a little bit, but it was more like he was talking, he was giving information. It seemed like a cerebral enough name for them."

Zieve showed the Heads "Artists Only," a song he had written in an earlier band of his own. Byrne took Zieve's words and wrote new music to them. The Heads would record the song on their second album.

Byrne was also teaching Tina to play the bass. "What she was playing was pretty rudimentary," Turtletaub remembered. "She had played guitar before that, so I'm sure that David knew what he was doing. He knew how to get her to do what he wanted her to do. The thing about Chris and Tina is that they would do that."

But if Tina and Chris were willing to follow Byrne's musical direction, they also supported and encouraged him. Tina later said of the trio's relationship, "We held David's hand."

"In the beginning," Tina said, "David didn't know if he

should be the singer. His vocal range is real high. I think it's because his head is real small. It's like a little gourd. It has a higher harmonic than my voice, a real high pitch. When we started his voice wasn't so good. But we talked about it and we said, 'David should sing.'

"We wanted to have the focus be on one person. Although the band was always collaborative, it was the kind of collaboration that exists between friends. We wanted people to have one person to focus on. It annoyed us that in some bands there was always someone else showing off. Just at the moment when the singer was saying something important or getting really impassioned, the bass player would start pumping his ass up and down. We didn't want that to happen.

"We thought people should concentrate on something very specific: David's writing and singing."

Talking Heads never followed a conscious plan on the order of groups like Devo, Chris Frantz claims. "But we knew that we weren't going to use the traditional methods of getting songs across: We weren't playing in that real heavy style or dressing in real sexy costumes or expecting David to run around like Mick Jagger."

For all their ambition, though, Byrne was still a movie usher, Tina was selling shoes and stationery at Bendel's department store, and Chris was a gofer at Design Research. It would be months before Byrne would deem his band ready to play their first gig.

"I had an allowance of five dollars a day," Tina said, "that I could spend on cigarettes, newspapers, books, transportation, and food. We weren't getting a proper diet. We were eating too many noodles. We were eating pasta every day and cheese instead of meat. That's all we could afford. It was so great when someone would ask us to dinner. When they'd invite us, we'd be even more of a burden, because we'd ask them if we could take a shower or a bath. We'd go to these parties and we'd say, 'Can I take a bath in your tub?' That was the worst thing—not having hot water and a toilet. And cooking on a hot plate is so awful."

But they were developing as a band. "David would always work the songs over," Zieve recalled. "He'd put things in, take things out, change it until the song they'd play was much different from the original." Many of their rehearsals were devoted to Byrne's changing songs. "The words would remain pretty much the same, but he might change the rhythm, the chords, the whole structure of the song. From the time he originally wrote 'Psycho Killer' until it was recorded, he worked it over ten or fifteen times. It became a different song."

Zieve said David employed a cheap rhythm box in early rehearsals. "He had a riot with that rhythm box," Zieve explained. "He used to fool around with it and get all these crazy rhythms going. He'd set up a certain rhythm, play his guitar with it, and then have Chris join in on drums. You can see what evolved from that. Their music has a lot to do with overlapping rhythms."

It's striking how Zieve's description of the construction of the earliest Talking Heads material was reflected, a decade later, in the band's concert film *Stop Making Sense*. That movie opened with Byrne alone on stage, playing "Psycho Killer" to the accompaniment of a taped rhythm track. One by one, musicians joined him on stage until, by adding a little at a time, the sound was transformed.

By January 1975, Byrne's attention was well focused on Talking Heads. Chris and Tina might not have been soulmates to Byrne, but they had given him support, a direction, and a goal worth working toward. Imagine what a jolt it must have been when he opened his mail and found an invitation from Andrea Kovacs to come up to Yale for her art exhibit.

"I had a huge exhibition," Andrea explained. "And much of the work was David: David's body, David doing this or that. I thought, 'Oh, I should invite him up to the show.' But what I really wanted was all his great albums to play for the opening. I didn't tell *him* that. I invited him up.

"He came up to New Haven by himself. I was up there with a whole entourage of followers: people from New York, people from Yale. I had photographs of my vagina being pulled open by my own dark fingernails, skin being squeezed and cracked and twisted. I called part of my show 'Love and Death by Attrition.' There was a whole twenty-by-forty-foot mural of David, with me touching his body parts.

"I was in this whirlwind. David came up—and I ignored the fact that he was there. I never once said hello to him. So he went and sat underneath his mural for the whole length of the show. And then he went home."

3

It was June 1975 before Byrne decided Talking Heads were
ready to audition at CBGB. The trio's rehearsals had
stretched into marathons, with friends coming by to offer
opinions. Jeff Turtletaub recalled watching the band re-
hearse the day before their debut: "David was taking us
down the elevator and he asked what I thought of the name,
if I thought they were ready."

"I don't know, David," Turtletaub replied. "It's kinda
weird."

The group was understandably nervous but, apparently,
performed well. The club's owner, Hilly Kristal, liked them
immediately and offered them a shot that night opening for
the Ramones, the prototypical punk band and CBGB favorites.

"Chris, the drummer, was as good as most, better than
others," Kristal explained. "David may not have known his
instrument well, but I don't think you could criticize him:
what he did play he played well. And he taught Tina. Tina
may not have been a bass player, but she learned to play
whatever she had to play as well as any professional."

Winning the gig at CBGB was the first triumph of the
Heads' career. Rock history has implied that the club was
an obscure bar when the Heads began, but in fact CBGB
was already emerging as a focal point for New York rock.

The club was dark and narrow, with a long bar running

along one wall and pool tables in the back. Outside bums and winos wandered the Bowery looking for windshields to wipe in exchange for handouts. If some bands who played there resented the grimy atmosphere, others were oblivious to it, and some took secret pride in just how funky they were.

The prototype for all CBGB bands was Lou Reed's Velvet Underground, marrying musical minimalism to lyrics about urban street life. Reed came from a literary background—he'd studied poetry with Delmore Schwartz—that tied his work into the Greenwich Village tradition of Burroughs and Ginsberg and, for that matter, Bob Dylan. The Velvet Underground disbanded in the early seventies, but different aspects of their influence were picked up by such underground bands as Boston's Modern Lovers, Detroit's Stooges, and the New York Dolls.

The Velvet Underground also influenced such British glitter rockers as David Bowie, who were considerably more successful than their American cousins at attracting large audiences.

The hippie ethic had led, in the early seventies, to American rock audiences embracing pastoral soft rock. The cities were out, nature was in. California songwriters such as Joni Mitchell, Jackson Browne, and the Eagles wrote from a perspective about as far from Lou Reed's Lower East Side mentality as one could get.

By the time Talking Heads debuted, though, the American disciples of the Velvet Underground were gaining commercial momentum. Reed himself enjoyed commercial success with "Walk on the Wild Side," a Bowie-produced single about Manhattan's gay subculture, and *Rock 'n' Roll Animal,* a live album on which he recast Velvet's songs in a slickly executed hard-rock format.

The reestablishment of urban rock & roll as a hip alternative to West Coast folk-rock was given a further boost by the emergence of Bruce Springsteen. Springsteen made a name for himself on the New York folk scene in 1973, but as quickly as he was signed by Columbia Records he revealed his rock & roll heart. Wearing black leather jackets on stage and singing about New York streets, subways, and fire escapes, Springsteen spent 1974 building a fanatical cult following in the Northeast. When the Heads played their first show in June 1975, Springsteen fever was building toward the explosion that would come in October, with the release of his LP *Born to Run.* Springsteen was soon on the covers of both *Time* and *Newsweek,* and New York street poets were crawling out of every manhole. Critics described Springsteen's image and music as "punk rock," although a few years later, after the British explosion of the Sex Pistols and the Clash, revisionist historians decided that "punk rock" was born without parents in 1976 or 1977. The revisionists stripped pre–Patti Smith acts like Reed and Springsteen of their punkdom.

In June 1975, CBGB was, as one of the few clubs open to unsigned original bands, an important showcase. When the Heads first appeared there, poet/rocker Patti Smith was already close to signing with Arista Records, the Ramones' three-chord thrashes were attracting lots of fans, and some writers were talking about punk.

"When Talking Heads started playing at CBGB," Wayne Zieve said, "it was already becoming so trendy that, in a way, you were an instant success if you just played there."

The Talking Heads weren't going to take any chances on not getting across to the CBGB audience either. They brought lots of friends to their first gigs.

The Weymouths were connected by marriage to the Grahams of the *Washington Post/Newsweek* dynasty. Tina's then-sister-in-law, Katherine Graham's daughter, was a *New*

York magazine writer, Lally Weymouth. Her brother was well connected with the New York music-art scene. From the start, the Heads drew a hip crowd.

But Turtletaub didn't think the band's press connections had much to do with the unprecedented newspaper attention the Heads' early shows generated.

"There wasn't anything else going on for the press to write about," he said. "It was just one of the advantages of Chris and Tina that they came with this extended family."

The *Village Voice* put the Heads on page one, as examples of New York's new underground scene. The article stated that the Talking Heads represented a "conservative impulse" in rock. A couple of years later, when the Heads were viewed as proto–New Wave, that assertion seemed ludicrous. A decade later, when the early Heads did indeed look like prototypical preppies/yuppies, that original *Voice* perspective seemed pretty canny. The *Voice* cover, which got a lot more attention than the content of the article, was quickly followed by glowing praise from John Rockwell in the *New York Times* and mention as part of a "new wave" in *Rolling Stone.* To the rock press, most of whom were young, white, college-educated, and progressive-minded, the Heads were naturally appealing. They were intellectual (for rockers), original, witty, and avant-garde but not, unlike some punk rockers, personally threatening.

The Heads had fashioned an image so straight as to be, among the longhairs and leather, attention-grabbing. Byrne and Chris wore Hush Puppies and Izod (or imitation Izod) shirts. Old friends of the band still disagree as to whether this was, as Byrne maintained, an attempt to be as nondescript as possible and focus all attention on the music, or, rather, the one sure way to get noticed in a self-consciously wild scene. Either way, those who saw Byrne as conservative and inhibited would have been shocked to realize that he'd already been punk—bleached hair and all—long before anyone had a name for it. Those who pegged Byrne as a young conservative might have been startled if they'd known that he was the child of liberal parents. For Byrne, adopting a conservative demeanor was a pretty revolutionary move. Wearing a LaCoste shirt to CBGB was a total contradiction in terms.

If their clothes were conservative, their act was surprising. "The first time I saw them," punk rocker Joey Ramone remembered, "David stuck out the most. He used to do these weird things with his eyes. He'd roll his eyes around and make chicken noises."

A friend named Diane Terenana recalled the dawn of the Talking Heads' public career: "When David sang, his eyes would dart around in an almost insane manner—wide open and darting from nervousness. Then all of a sudden the *Village Voice* comes out and says, 'Go see this band, it's wonderful. David Byrne is so intense that his eyes dart around like Ping-Pong balls.' Well, David immediately broke himself of that habit. He never did it again after that article."

"What made for their crisp, New Wave image," Jamie Dalglish said, "was also being able to come across the street from CBGB and take a shower here before the second set. They were always very polite. Chris would always call up and say 'How are you?' before he'd start asking me for something."

The cerebral Heads might have seemed a strange opening act for the black-leather-jacketed Ramones, who blasted primitive power chords while chanting songs like, "Now I Wanna Sniff Some Glue," "Blitzkreig Bop," and "Chain Saw." The New York–bred Ramones were, visually and culturally, worlds apart from their art-school support act. But the Ramones fans accepted the Heads immediately— more enthusiastically, in fact, than they accepted punk bands who copied the Ramones' Gabba-Gabba approach.

"Hilly brought them in to open for us," said Tommy Erdelyi, the band's drummer under the name of Tommy Ramone. "Right away we saw that it worked. After that, whenever we had to find someone to play with us, we'd use the Talking Heads. Even though the Ramones played hard and raunchy, conceptually there were a lot of similarities: the minimalism. Even though their music was totally different, the concept was similar. We were so unique at the time that they were the first ones who played with us who actually fit."

"David could create a wall," said Dalglish. "He could be invisible. At CBGB, he could walk through a room full of people after doing this tremendously charged performance and look like he wasn't even there. He'd disappear.

"But when David performed he was electric. You could feel the subways under his feet. The keenest statement David made about music at that time was that it could be done minimally, with three people, and they could really evoke this kind of electrical charge."

Within months CBGB was packed for every Heads performance. Fans would attempt to join them on stage and sing along. Yet the band always seemed in control of their situation.

"Other bands would get up and put it all out there," Dalglish points out, "and throw things at the audience. And then the Talking Heads, all very reserved looking, would come on, sit down at the drums, pick up the bass, and come out with this minimalist sound that was just electrifying. David would get up with the audience all rioting, and he would get on stage and quiet everything down. It was almost like someone reaching out and reclaiming land or laws or loyalty or admiration. You couldn't help but like it."

"They were definitely different," said Fred Smith, who played bass with Television, one of the best of the CBGB bands. "You didn't know what David, with his special voice and jerky movements, would do next. They were a very full-sounding band for a three-piece. I really liked Tina's simplicity on the bass. After seeing them I went out and bought a Mustang bass like hers. All the guys went to see the cute blonde."

"When Tina first came to New York, all the guys were chasing after her," said Dee Dee Ramone. "She was very popular. Nobody could tell if she was Chris's girlfriend or not. I think they didn't want to tell. A lot of times, if people in bands are married, they don't tell. Except for Elvis Presley."

'In the early days," Tina said, "there were only a handful of people who used to go down to CBGB. Maybe, all told, five hundred people in New York knew about it the first year. So it was the same people going down, and those people were artists and early punks. They were people who were looking for something new, and they saw the ideas in the bands on stage. And they could see they were really good ideas. But it wasn't a completely formed thing. It wasn't a finished presentation, and a lot of people started writing about it before it was finished because they were so fascinated by the ideas being presented."

"When they started getting famous," Dalglish said, "they would come over here and Chris would be reading the newspaper. And if he noticed something about Talking Heads there was this electricity.

"It wasn't an ego trip with David. He never broadcast the publicity he was getting. There were a lot of bands around, but Talking Heads soon took the lead. There were a lot of character types around, like Richard Hell. David would always play with these people."

Sometimes Byrne seemed distant, detached. But then his sense of humor would come through. Once Dalglish came home to find Susan's eyebrows plucked and Byrne, the plucker, with the uprooted hairs laid out on a napkin in perfect eyebrow shape.

Dalglish and Susan decided to marry. They went up to Providence for the wedding, which was attended by most of the old RISD crowd. Talking Heads were the wedding band. They played three one-hour sets, including covers of "Love Is All Around" by Tina's teenage favorites, the Troggs, and "96 Tears," David and Andrea's song.

It was summer. Yale was over. Andrea Kovacs came back to New York and took a loft in Chinatown. Soon she and David were back together. But Andrea, who had been the star of the relationship with Byrne the summer before, was startled to find that while she had been at school he had become a local celebrity: "David no longer sought a solution out of proximity to me or through love," she observed. "He had started to grow, to evolve, to spring full-form from that mattress he was lying on. He'd connected with Chris and Tina, and I think they'd taken my place with him.

"Things got defensive now that I was back on the scene. I think Tina really loved David, too. They were so close and working together so much. David sculpted Tina's entire style and taught her everything, so there was so much love there in that regard. She allowed her whole being to become his art form.

"David told me there was no personal interest between him and those people, that it was a working relationship. They were very devoted to him in terms of the group, but I got the feeling that he was very much a loner, even in the group. But he would stay with me, and we had the most wonderful summer in Chinatown."

Still, having gone AWOL once, Andrea found it more difficult than she expected to reenlist.

"Tina was an exciting woman to be with," she said. "But

Tina was also a very competitive woman, and much stronger than I was. She was much more confident. I started to feel a little insecure around her, rather nudged to the side.

"I'm a big woman and Tina's slight. I noticed that David, over that period of time, started to get smaller and smaller physically. The year before, he'd given me the impression of virility and strength. By the time he was with Tina and Chris for several months, he had gotten very diminished."

Andrea said she told Byrne she felt like an outsider, and he asked her if she wanted to join the band as keyboard player. She was delighted he asked but wouldn't consider sacrificing her own budding career as an art photographer to play rock & roll with her boyfriend. She was also a bit uncomfortable with the notion of being, officially, David's sideman. Although she had surrendered the idea of superiority in romance with Byrne, Andrea was still lobbying for equality.

She recalled the first time she went to CBGB, where she and David had spent a summer watching other bands, to see Talking Heads play. "It was such a sensational feeling. It was like being in the eye of the hurricane. Being David's girl-friend at the heart, at the center of this scene, was a quintes-sential experience. At the end of the performance, Chris got into it so much he fell off his drum stool backward."

At the end of the evening the group returned to the loft on Christie Street and counted their money. They'd made eighty dollars. Andrea was impressed but also threatened by David's nascent self-sufficiency. Later, she moved into the loft that David, Chris, and Tina shared, where her outsider's status became increasingly apparent. "The three of them were really a group. Tina would do things like give David a massage by walking on his back. I couldn't do that. I would've crushed him. I felt like I was starting to not be part of it anymore."

What followed was like *A Clockwork Orange,* in which

all the bad things the narrator did in the first part of the book came back to haunt him in the second: Andrea began moping around, complaining that her artistic career wasn't moving quickly enough. Byrne's reply was, "Get off your high horse and get a job."

"He said to me exactly what I had said to him," she recalled. "He was giving me the same treatment. I got a miserable job, and my self-esteem started to tumble down, down, down, while David's was starting to build, build, build. I became the weaker one, clinging to him like a comet taking off."

The final blow came when Byrne told her, "I don't get your jokes anymore." So one day, when the others were out, Andrea packed up her things and went. She left behind, on David's bed, a large photograph of herself sleeping.

"We had day jobs," Tina said. "And we kept thinking, 'It's gonna be so great when the only kind of work we have to do is the band.' It was real hard to play in the clubs till four in the morning and then have to get up at eight. You just wouldn't go to bed. It was just crazy. The only time you weren't moving was when you were asleep.

"The band became this big loyalty thing. It's like chivalry; you have a sense of honor. You get to feel very, very loyal. It's like a family. But you know, if we didn't have success we'd probably break up."

"The one thing that made Talking Heads," Hilly Kristal said, "aside from the talent, is that they concentrated. They knew what their musical structure was, they seemed to have a goal, and they went for it, right from the beginning. They became very strong."

Joey Ramone recalled that on warm summer nights in 1975 all the CBGB people—bands and audience—would hang around the cars outside the club before the shows started.

There were jealousies and competition but, especially among the bands who were breaking out, also a camaraderie.

The Patti Smith Group had already pulled away from the pack. Guitarist Lenny Kaye recalled watching Talking Heads build momentum.

"I first saw Talking Heads opening for the Ramones," he said. "The initial interest was Tina, very determined, playing bass. This wasn't a standard girl role in rock & roll; she wasn't singing or dancing.

"Chris and Tina, the rhythm section, were really central. Talking Heads were a dance band. When I first used to go visit them at their loft they used to talk about Bohannon all the time. It was a great reference, especially since 'dance music' had a totally different connotation for avant-garde rockers in those days. That element of blackness can't be underestimated. And it stemmed from the rhythm section."

In 1975 the fermenting punk scene thought of itself as diametrically opposed to funk and disco, the slick black styles that were increasingly dominating nightclubs and Top 40 radio. Talking Heads didn't yet have the chops to make it obvious, but they were already attracted to black grooves. "They just got better and better and better," Kaye explained. "Pretty soon the highs of the set had tipped the balance, and you had a group who knew what they were doing. It was a gradual accumulation of experience and confidence. They'd become a real band. It's almost like you see a little girl next door, and you walk by one day and she's suddenly grown up."

Late in summer 1975, the Ramones signed a contract with Sire Records. Sire was an independent label run by Seymour Stein, a native New Yorker with a collector's enthusiasm for rock & roll. Stein had a good ear; he could spot trends coming. As a young fan in the early sixties, he'd been amazed when major American labels passed on distribution rights to great new British recordings. Stein watched as Capitol gave up its option on the second Beatles single and let a small label grab it. Even after that remarkable goof was rectified, Stein noticed how many great foreign bands were missed by American giants.

In the late sixties, Stein launched Sire Records, and for the next six years the company pretty much devoted its attention to domestic licensing of British groups. By the late seventies, Sire was best known as a cultist label that reissued such British Invasion favorites as the Searchers. In 1973, though, the label had a great stroke of fortune with the unexpected commercial success of the European progressive rock band Focus. That windfall gave Stein a bit more capital to work with and established Sire as more than an oldies label.

The Ramones had a lot of the spirit of the British Invasion bands Stein loved, and their manager, Danny Fields, shared some of Stein's New York fan/collector interests.

"I'll never forget the night I went down to see the Ramones." Stein said, his enthusiasm still clear. "It was 1975 and it was autumn, a beautiful night. The opening act was supposed to be the Shirts, whom I had no desire to see. We were standing outside when all of a sudden I heard, 'When my love stands next to your love,' " the opening of Byrne's "Love Goes to a Building on Fire."

"I was picked up by the music like a piece of dust by a carpet sweeper. I was swept into the club almost backward. I saw these people on stage. David was singing. He was a decent guitar player even then. I'd never seen movements like his before. Then you had Tina, the bass player. Her eyes were like a Keane painting. She was transfixed on David's every move. Chris was cooking away, doing a very good job, but the main interplay was between David and Tina.

"At the end of the show, there was no crew, nothing. This poor, beautiful girl was helping Chris take the drums off stage."

Stein approached the band, introduced himself, and said he wanted to sign them to his label. They invited him back to their loft and talked. The Heads were gracious but not anxious to sign a record deal. They didn't feel they were ready.

This reluctance to sign was Talking Heads' riskiest, most unusual, and, in the long run, probably single most important decision. Rock bands dream of being offered record deals, and CBGB was, by that autumn, especially competitive. Some good bands play for years without ever attracting an offer, and hardly any will turn down one deal if they don't have another deal pending.

But Talking Heads were smart enough to be restrained. Lots of rock acts sign bad deals and are never promoted at all; if an album doesn't create a stir on its own, the record company uses it as a tax write-off. Other bands are kept in thrall to a label, the advance money they are unable to repay hung over their heads to force them to comply with the label's notion of what's commercial. Talking Heads weren't going to let any of the old familiar horror stories happen to them.

For almost a full year after Stein's initial offer, they continued to perform locally, to attract fans and the press, and to perfect their songs and stage act. Big record labels began sniffing around, too. The Heads were polite, went out to dinner with executives, talked business—and at first made no promises.

They continued to work at day jobs. They had no manager. They did not let themselves be tempted by quick cash or big talk. Considering that their music was far from main-stream, that north of Fourteenth Street the whole punk movement was scoffed at as a silly fad, Talking Heads that year showed nerves of steel.

Lou Reed himself told RCA it should sign the band.

Capitol Records came around. So did Columbia. Seymour Stein was getting more and more nervous that Talking Heads would be scooped up by a major. But the Heads hadn't forgotten Sire. A small label, as David Byrne told Mary Clarke, was far more likely to pay attention to the Heads. A big label might forget they were there.

"Maybe the record company would just keep us on their label and let us make records as a prestige act, since the press had been real kind to us," Tina observed. "Maybe they'd keep us just because it would make their business seem less . . . mercenary."

The Heads asked manager Danny Fields if the Ramones were happy with Sire. He said they were.

"I told them there wasn't going to be much cash," Fields said. "There wouldn't be suitcases full of dollar bills on the doorstep. But they would see the royalties and have artistic control of everything, from packaging to product. I told them Seymour was wonderful. You couldn't ask for a more giving, understanding, and appreciative person at a record company. I'd seen them all."

Finally, in summer 1976, Byrne calmed Stein by telling him, "Don't worry. We've given you our word."

They made sure that their deal with Sire gave them creative control, and then they signed.

Whether because of Byrne's Scottish frugality or Chris's and Tina's relatively sophisticated background, the Heads crafted a sensible economic strategy.

"We always had a real neat way of going about our business," Tina said. "We decided we would never be in debt.

Don't take money in advance that you couldn't pay back. This was our way of getting around having our arms twisted, of maintaining artistic control."

"The first thing David bought when they signed," Mary Clarke said, "was a color TV set. He didn't go out and buy a million things. He'd been poor for so long he was really careful with money. He bought lots of records. He felt good about it, but he certainly didn't go overboard in any way."

Mary and David were getting to be better friends. She had been close to Andrea in the months after the breakup and had heard her lamentations about blowing a good thing. Andrea was crushed when she found out that Mary was David's new girlfriend.

"It was a normal relationship," Mary explained. "Like everyone else we went out to dinner, we went to movies, we went to a few parties. There was nothing exotic about it."

"David and that whole circle of RISD people would sit around reading topical magazines," said Andrea. "There would be no speaking, just gathering information."

Andrea wasn't positive "The Book I Read" was about Mary, but she knew David had written a song about *her:* "No Compassion."

Sire Records was moving from a distribution deal with the shaky ABC to one with mighty Warner Brothers Records. Seymour Stein knew that it would be in the best interests of Talking Heads to hold up their first album until after that shift was made. But there was a chance of sending the Heads to Britain as a support act for the Ramones in the spring if they could get something released in Europe quickly.

So, in December 1976, Byrne, Chris, and Tina went into a Manhattan studio and cut a single of "Love Goes to a Building on Fire," the song that had mesmerized Stein that first night at CBGB. The trio's sparse sound needed some bolstering, and the producer, Tony Bongiovi, decided that *horns* would be just the thing.

The Heads, their love for black music eternal, wanted the brass to have a Stax/Volt punch, but it came out sounding thin and slightly classical, like the horns on the Beatles' "Penny Lane." The record vanished without a trace in America, but when placed with music writers and agents in England, it helped secure the Ramones tour for Talking Heads, as well as a limited deal with, and advance money from, Phonogram, a major British label.

The minimal guitar/bass/drum format was obviously not going to be sufficient to make the jump from club shows to recording. Talking Heads needed a fourth member.

"It was pretty necessary," Lenny Kaye said. "As a trio their sound was one-dimensional, not a lot of color. Trios are very hard to work with. You sometimes need people to take that weight off."

There may have been another factor. Chris and Tina, always seen as a single unit, were by that spring engaged to be married. The two people who claimed to have rejected earlier offers to join Talking Heads—Kehoe and Andrea— were both intimates of Byrne with a slight connection to Chris and Tina. Jerry Harrison, who'd first sat in with the band the previous September, was perceived by friends as being closer to Byrne than to the others.

"I think it was good for David to have Jerry," Mary Clarke said. "I think it balanced things in terms of, shall we say, power plays. Jerry and David kind of paired off. David and I had very little to do with Chris and Tina socially, but once Jerry came into the picture we'd do stuff with him and his girlfriend, Linda.

"The feeling was that they had a really good musician, and they were happy. I think Jerry read music. He was seen as a really good addition."

Harrison didn't officially join Talking Heads until April

1977, a year after he first saw the band and six months after he began playing occasional dates with them. The long courtship was largely the result of Harrison's playing hard to get. While the Heads negotiated their deal and recorded their first single, Harrison was sticking to a decision to get through Harvard. Rock stardom had lured him away from the Ivy League once before.

Harrison, who grew up in the Midwest, had been a keyboard player with the Modern Lovers, a Boston band whose spare sound and observational lyricism represent the missing link between the Velvet Underground and Talking Heads. But Jonathan Richman, Modern Lovers' singer/songwriter/guitarist, was a genuinely straight suburban kid. Unlike Byrne, Jonathan had always been upright and clean-living, the kind of fellow Wally Cleaver would have been proud to call a pal.

Richman had been a teenage fan of the Velvet Underground and had even made a pilgrimage to New York to get to know them. But while he loved their musical sparseness, Jonathan had little use for lyrics about heroin. In a counter-revolution predating Byrne's by at least four years, Richman sang the praises of old-fashioned values.

Harrison and his Harvard roommate Ernie Brooks met Jonathan in the 1970–71 school year, when he wandered into a Cambridge party they were giving with a bunch of Andy Warhol cronies, associates from his Lou Reed hegira. At the time, Harrison was a good-looking Harvard undergraduate with radical politics and a gift for all sorts of art: design, filmmaking, and music.

"I was making a movie at this time," Harrison explained, "and Jonathan's whole rap—he really had his rap together —about the beauty of commercial enterprises, the signs on the highway, and Howard Johnson's fit in with the idea I had for this movie.

"I filmed and recorded a number of his performances.

Ernie and I were talking and we said, 'There's something here that's really great!' So Jonathan came over and started talking about whether we would play with him. First Ernie joined and then about a week or two later I joined." And so the Modern Lovers was set: Jonathan on guitar and vocals, Jerry on keyboards, Ernie on bass, and David Robinson (who would later help form the Cars) on drums.

Jonathan lined up some gigs in the suburbs; city jobs fell to Harrison and Brooks. Jerry also landed some Harvard mixers that didn't go over too well: "They wanted to hear the Rolling Stones, rhythm and blues. We definitely didn't give 'em what they wanted for their dances. We developed this incredibly chauvinistic attitude that there was no other music in the world worth listening to except the Modern Lovers. No one else was carrying on the faith."

No one was hiring them, either. The Lovers were barely scraping by; Jonathan's parents would regularly donate Care packages of food. But the band's dogged individualism and willingness to play anywhere—including, once, a tourist hotel in Bermuda—kept their legend alive.

Danny Fields, who'd known Jonathan from his days in New York, came up to see the Lovers and brought with him *New York Daily News* critic Lillian Roxon. After Roxon wrote a short rave about the Modern Lovers, record companies were flying in from all over to see them.

"It was very funny," Harrison said, "because all these people were coming up to see us, all these articles were being written, and we were really broke. People took us out to really great meals, and we'd have no money to eat for the rest of the week. It was like being a camel. You'd try to eat as much as you could when you went out so you could make it to the next time someone was going to take you out."

Most Boston bands at this time were into blues rock—the J. Geils Band was king—and many were appalled to see record companies pursuing this bizarre ensemble. But the Lovers convinced two of them, Warner's and A&M, to pay their way to the West Coast, land of the emerging Eagles/ Jackson Browne sound.

The trip to California was a disaster. The band did two sets of demos there, one for each of the two record companies. Warner's sessions were produced by the Velvet Underground's John Cale, and this demo eventually emerged as the first Modern Lovers album. Their newly acquired managers, Shifman and Larson—whose big act was soft rockers Loggins and Messina—dropped out after seeing the group booed and pelted while opening for Tower of Power. They were replaced by Phil Kaufman, Gram Parsons's aide-de-camp, who became the Lovers' unofficial road manager. This association involved the group with Parsons, the brilliant ex-Byrd and Flying Burrito who died soon after, as well as Emmylou Harris, his harmony singer. The Modern Lovers moved into their vacated house. The group was in San Francisco when Parsons died in 1973. Newspapers were soon full of headlines about the theft of the singer's body and its subsequent cremation in the desert.

"Everyone was so conscious of 'Manson fever,' " Harrison recalled. "Then Phil showed up giggling, and we realized *our road manager did it!*"

When it came out that Kaufman had been obeying Parson's wishes in not letting his body be sent home, Parsons's family sued for grand theft. The Modern Lovers played a benefit to pay off the coffin.

All this craziness was taking its toll. Jonathan and David were fighting all the time. Jonathan decided he did not want to perform any of his old songs. This horrified Warner Brothers, who wanted assurances that the band would tour to support the album.

The group returned to Boston without Robinson, who

was fed up. Jonathan wanted to play softer music, which sat poorly with Harrison and Brooks. Bob Turner, a high school friend of Harrison's, came in on drums. The Modern Lovers found that their fame had grown while they had been away, that now they were a hot local band. But the split was irreversible. The band broke up in February 1974.

Following his experience with the Modern Lovers, Harrison continued playing in bands for a while—at one point he and Ernie Brooks toured and recorded with Elliot Murphy, a promising, would-be rock star of the moment—but finally decided to give up music and return to grad school. After sending in all his deposits, he received the call to join Talking Heads. Jerry had been around long enough to know it was a good deal. Still, he hesitated.

"There was one point when I was considering joining, and I thought, 'There's something really spare and pure about this threesome, and if I join it's not going to be as spare.' Then I thought, 'Well, if they want me to join, and I think it's going to sound better, okay. I don't have to worry about it.' "

After completing his semester, Jerry joined the band for good. He felt fortunate that he wasn't replacing anyone else, that he could come up with his own keyboard ideas rather than have to learn established parts. When there was no obvious need for a new part, he would double Tina's bass or reinforce Byrne's guitar. Harrison himself had taken up guitar, which gave him a chance to work into songs that needed no keyboards at all. He also began singing background parts.

If a few old Heads fans were put off by the expansion, it made the sound accessible to many more. What had often been a sort of conceptual sketch of a rock group became a working model. Harrison came in as a bit of a hired gun. The other three had their names on the recording contract. He didn't.

"At first I was probably much less rigid than the others," Harrison said, "because I'd played in other bands and I knew other philosophies could work. I had been at the point of giving up, and I took what I thought was a professional attitude. I thought, 'I just want to make this as good as possible and I think I know how I'm going to do it.' I didn't mind feeling limited, because I thought that was the professional thing to do."

At first Harrison played on only a few songs. The rest of the time he sat in a chair.

Harrison had another, nonmusical function in Talking Heads as they began zeroing in on an expanded market: Bullishly handsome, with a halo of curly hair, he *looked* like a rock star.

"Real small kids have no trouble with Talking Heads music," Tina said in 1979, "but people who are used to typical rock and rollers have to get used to us. That's why it's good to have Jerry; he gives them what they want.

"Some people think Jerry *is* the bandleader because he *swans.*" (To swan is to lean back, eyes half-shut, as if in ecstasy.) "None of us know how to swan, but Jerry's been in other groups before, so he does. It's because he's excited. He's probably thinking about food more than sex. He's probably thinking about what he's going to eat after the show."

Talking Heads started work on an album as soon as Harrison joined, but put it on hold in order to go to Europe with the Ramones. During that tour, Harrison's position as fourth Head was solidified.

Jamie Dalglish recalled, "Talking Heads found Jerry, and then Jerry was their best friend. He was very closemouthed. It almost seemed like a carny atmosphere. They wouldn't let out what was going on; they wouldn't bitch; they wouldn't complain. They really had things under control."

The Ramones tour, Talking Heads' first European engagement, began in late April 1977. The Ramones had been to England before; if it's an oversimplification to say that their first visit to the United Kingdom set off the British punk explosion, it's an oversimplification that's nevertheless been accepted as truth.

In fact, Joey Ramone has said, "I feel we were responsible for the whole punk revolution. We signed to Sire in 1975 and our first album came out in 1976. It came out in England about six months before it came out in America. That's sort of what inspired the English bands to start up. When we first went over there the big thing was pub rock."

The Ramones' return to Britain—and their first crack at Switzerland, France, Belgium, and Holland—would turn out to be a cause for great excitement in the emerging European punk culture. Still, the British musical establishment had to be convinced that a Ramones tour was a hot prospect.

Ed Bicknell was working for NEMS, a British booking agency, when his old friend Ken Kushnik called from America to ask if he would be interested in doing a tour with the Ramones.

Bicknell asked his wife, a successful publicist hipper than he, if she'd ever heard of the Ramones. She said, "Great, great! You should do it!" Then Kushnik explained that a second band called Talking Heads was included in the package. When Bicknell balked, Kushnik sent him a copy of the Heads' 45, "Love Goes to a Building on Fire." Bicknell loved the record, but he was even more struck by the photo on the sleeve: "I thought 'God, these people have got really long necks.' I was absolutely intrigued by the appearance of them."

Bicknell was also impressed that the Heads' song had an identifiable melody—something of a novelty at the dawn of punk. He agreed to book the tour.

The chance to surf along on that wave was a great boost for Talking Heads. It was also natural; the compatibility of the two bands had been established at CBGB, and they were now signed to the same record label. And showing up in the company of the Ramones bestowed on Talking Heads a credibility with punk audiences who might otherwise have looked askance at their Izod shirts and middle-class posture.

Bicknell first laid eyes on the band—now expanded to include guitarist/keyboardist Jerry Harrison—when they landed in Zurich. The agent was impressed by the contrast between Talking Heads and the Ramones.

The cultural distance between old rock and New Wave, the cultural distance between Europe and the USA, were as nothing when put next to the distance between the two groups' attitudes toward their new environment.

Danny Fields, their then-manager, recalled, "The Talking Heads were doing your Auntie Mame cultural bullshit tour of Europe. They wanted to see every ruin. The Talking Heads came from, how should we say, the *educated* classes, and while we love the Ramones, we know that they didn't.

"The Ramones hated Europe. They didn't like the idea that people didn't speak English. The Talking Heads adored it. It was really yuppie chic at work. The Ramones were like Archie Bunker at the Vatican. They were not amused. They hated the food and just looked for hamburgers everywhere. They were going to see American movies and even resented the French subtitles. The Heads were trying to lose themselves in the wonders of the Old World."

A feud developed between Johnny Ramone and Tina Weymouth. It started when Tina reportedly noted that the Talking Heads carried their own guitars while the Ramones relied on roadies. "Who," Tina allegedly asked, "do you think you are?"

"We're rock stars now," the Ramones replied. "We don't do that kind of stuff. We don't lift a thing. We're not the roadies. If you want to be like that, you can."

Relations aboard the tour bus were polite but not affectionate.

"The thing that struck me," Bicknell said, "was when we went for a meal. If I finished my main course, and there was maybe a half a piece of meat on the plate, one of the Ramones would grab it and eat it, because they had absolutely no money. Seymour Stein had them touring Europe on a daily allowance of three pounds per person per day. Of course, that wouldn't buy them an orange juice in Switzerland. But the Talking Heads were sitting there having a banquet. They all appeared to have some sort of private means. They've always been good at handling money. It showed even then."

"We were booked into the same hotels," Joey Ramone remembered. "But I don't think we hung out with them. It wasn't like we were a big happy family. They were more into the whole continental aspect. They would talk to everybody in French, and we sort of got pissed off about that." Joey laughed. "We didn't know what they were talking about."

"They used to do things like go to art galleries," Ed Bicknell explained. "They weren't trying to be pretentious. I remember, in Amsterdam, saying 'Where have you been today?' and they would say, 'We went to see the Van Gogh exhibit.' Now, most rock groups can't get up before four and then have horrible problems with their bowel movements."

"We didn't want to go sightseeing," explained Dee Dee Ramone, still adamant after all these years. "It was awful enough being over there. What is there to see? To go to Stonehenge you have to drive, like, two hundred miles out of the way down country roads. And when you get there, it's really nothing to see! It's not like going to see a *castle*. That would be worth it. But not a monument of primitive stone! We finally ended up having to go there and the Ramones didn't get out of the bus. They went and looked at it, and we sat on the bus."

"They were telling me on the bus they were going to play a gallery," Tommy (Ramone) Erdelyi remembered. "I said, 'Why are you playing galleries? You were art students, now you're rock and roll performers. I would think you'd want to get away from that kind of thing. You should play rock and roll venues.' They said, 'No, this is a good idea.' Well, little did I know that that was the perfect thing for them to do. Playing a gallery sort of set them off. They knew what they were doing."

The European punk audiences accepted Talking Heads right off the bat. But, as Danny Fields explained, "The Ramones got the hardcore, funkier audience and the Talking Heads got all the art students. I didn't know there were that many art students in Geneva. Each band had its own circle of groupies."

"Because of the type of charismatic personality David is, David attracted a certain type of female," Ed Bicknell recalled, "a girl who wants to know the meaning of a lyric. He would sit and smile and be amused by this attention, and then go pick up a sandwich and go to bed. He certainly wasn't a raver. He was just David. He was this strange little chap who delighted in the idea that people found him a little bit strange."

In concert the Heads performed in bright white light and did without traditional rock & roll stage props. Although David hadn't yet developed the kind of body movements that would make his presence so galvanizing in *Stop Making Sense*, he was still, Bicknell recalled, "an electric performer, and in the confines of the club your eyes would go to him. Then there was this little blond girl with a ponytail humping this vast bass. Tina used to watch David all the time with her big staring eyes. There was a sort of ESP between them, a sort of signal. Musically, they were very intense to me."

Byrne's eccentricity wasn't confined to the Heads' performances. "He would test the microphone by doing some kind of vocal exercises, almost birdlike noises," Tommy Erdelyi remembered. "People were mesmerized by it."

"David was starting to develop this strange persona which has become very interesting," said Bicknell. "He enjoys his eccentricity. I would observe him turning it on, particularly to journalists. He would play at being David Byrne. He tended to act out the image a lot."

While David was defining his persona as celebrity/artist, Chris and Tina were overseeing the financial development of Talking Heads. Tina often worked on the band's accounts, using a pad and pencil. "It was a small pot, but they were very aware of what was *in* the pot," Bicknell declares. "David was obviously the creative one, and I think he possibly intimidated Tina at the time. Tina wasn't technically a particularly good bass player. Chris was not Buddy Rich or Steve Gadd, but he had a great feel and he could pump it out. The thing I remember most about Jerry is that he seemed to be very interested in his appearance. He was always combing his hair or looking in mirrors, or at his reflection in darkened windows."

"They were different than us," Dee Dee Ramone said. "But I really grew fond of Chris and Tina. Jerry I liked, too. I didn't know David at all. They were so strange to me. We were into the Sex Pistols and the Damned and the MC5 and the Stooges, and they were into this whole funky thing. They were listening to Al Green and stuff like that."

That the Talking Heads were aficionados of black music was apparent to only the most perceptive of listeners. Byrne's hyper-Caucasian voice and the band's sometimes stiff rhythmic sense still sounded pretty white to a general audience. At that point Harrison was still playing a backseat role, and neither Byrne nor Tina were musically very versatile. In concert Chris's drums, the most dependable of the Heads' components, were pushed up in the mix to bolster the band's sonic kick. Obviously, this emphasis increased the drummer's influence on the other players. Chris was better capable of conveying a funk feeling than were David and Tina, and the dominance of his drums helped steer the developing band toward R&B grooves.

The subtle funk feeling gave the Heads, so quirky and oddball on record, an instant, familiar dance hook in live performance.

"Talking Heads were well liked all the time," Dee Dee points out, "and it's surprising 'cause other bands, like Television and Richard Hell, didn't go over too well. Television were great, but they just didn't play the right punk beat. The punk rock beat is a dance. Talking Heads were very danceable. They were very kooky. I think the kids looked at them and thought they were crazy."

Talking Heads skipped the Ramones' Scandinavian dates to go to England early for two shows at the Rock Garden, a tiny club in London's Covent Garden. By now the Heads had acquired a formidable reputation, at least in hip pop circles; the music press appeared in droves, and the club was packed. The Rock Garden show on May 14, 1977, spawned ecstatic articles in the British music papers. But the night had an even greater significance in the Heads' history. That was the show when John Cale (whose New York all-star

pickup band had featured David Byrne the summer before)
brought Brian Eno to see Talking Heads for the first time.
Eno had been keyboard player with Roxy Music, the
British art-school band Byrne had so admired. Eno later got
great mileage out of claiming to be more a theorist than a
musician, a boast that could legitimately be made by half the
rock musicians in the world, were they not so unenlightened
as to think such an admission embarrassing. Eno, however,
had been a self-proclaimed nonmusician since the late sixties. After leaving Roxy in 1973, Eno recorded conceptual,
instrumental albums of electronic background music. He
labeled these projects "ambient," as if all music were not
capable of ambience.

In the years ahead, Eno would become the band's producer, an unofficial fifth member, and, finally, the reason for
hard feelings and division.

"I remember being especially impressed by the approach
they took to their playing," Eno recalled of that first meeting. "David and Jerry together made a brilliant rhythm
guitarist, while Chris and Tina were perfectly poised between pop and soul. Altogether it was an approach to
rhythm which was rather unique—David/Jerry's edgy, spiky
guitar work over Tina's rolling, wavy bass lines over Chris's
powerful and solid drumming. It created a field of charged
rhythmic space—stark but tense, always slightly off-balance
and therefore always moving forward."

Hardly anybody in the punk scene thought like that.
Byrne and Eno began a correspondence. But aside from
Eno, the Heads expressed little fascination with the British
punk stars with whom they were suddenly rubbing elbows.
Tina thought Joe Strummer of the Clash was an old pub-
rocker lying about his age; and while they found most of the
Brits pleasant enough guys, they thought Johnny Rotten
made a special effort to be obnoxious.

When the Ramones arrived in Britain, the Heads rejoined them for a tour of universities and sweaty clubs. It was at the Roundhouse in London that Talking Heads had their first serious encounter with "gobbing"—the English punk craze of audience members spitting on the performers.

"The Ramones used to get it," Bicknell recalled. "I remember in Liverpool the audience was six inches from the faces of the Ramones. During the performance the people in the front row spit directly into the faces of Johnny and Dee Dee, much to their irritation. Johnny Ramone would just yell abuse at the audience. He'd threaten to come down and hit them with his guitar. Joey would just pull his hair over his face."

But Talking Heads pretty much avoided that. In London, Bicknell remembered, there was "a sea of gob" from the audience, but the Heads, though probably surprised, showed no reaction. And for the most part, the gobbers left the Heads alone. "Possibly the spitters were lurking in the back during their set," Tommy Erdelyi speculated. "But I don't think so. They just didn't make you wanna spit."

The soundman assigned to both bands was a Scotsman named Frank Gallagher, who had never heard of either the Ramones or Talking Heads. Still, he later related, "After the first sound check I went back to the hotel with Chris and Tina and said, 'I don't know what it is, but I want in.' "

"I never saw them fail with an audience. I never saw them die, ever. Even if you weren't into the way they looked you could still get off on the passion coming off the stage."

Musical familiarity led to Harrison's opening up more, finding parts that didn't follow Byrne's guitar or Tina's bass so closely. Just as soldiers who've been through boot camp together become lifelong pals, Harrison benefited from having been with David, Chris, and Tina as they began their ascent.

Talking Heads returned to America in a state of professional grace. They had won audiences everywhere and had become darlings of the frequently snide and fickle British music press. There would certainly be future tours of England, and on those tours Talking Heads would certainly headline.

The band had no problem adapting to their new celebrity.

"They were at ease with what was happening," Tommy Erdelyi explained. "They were in their medium somehow."

The week after Talking Heads returned from Europe, on June 18, 1977, Chris and Tina were married in Washington, Kentucky, the town Chris's family considered home.

None of the Providence expatriate crowd around Dalglish's house was invited to the wedding. They were miffed, especially considering that the guest list did include such new friends as Seymour Stein and his wife; Ken Kushnik, Sire's director of artistic development; and Jerry Harrison and his girlfriend, Linda. The old RISD pals were starting to get the idea that the Heads would not be bringing along hitchhikers on their drive to glory.

Mary Clarke recalled, "Even though I had been going out with David for months, I was not invited. David insisted on bringing me. That put everyone in a funny position. David went out to Brooks Brothers and bought a seersucker suit. I got some kind of shift dress. It was very, very hot, even for the South. I thought my going had been cleared beforehand, but Tina looked surprised when I showed up, so I don't think it was.

"There were so many relatives. Everyone was very polite. I'm not a WASP, so it was kind of foreign to me. There was a rehearsal dinner and this dinner and that dinner; there seemed to be a series of meals that we had to keep going to. It was a whole weekend of events. I remember going on a house tour in the town. It was just one thing after another in this really unbearable heat.

"David and I were late for the wedding. We came in, sat down, and there they were. Tina had on a beautiful dress. She looked beautiful. Chris had a suit on. It was a beautiful church, very formal. It was the world's longest wedding.

"There was a dinner at Chris's grandmother's beautiful old house. I remember sitting on the porch and a band started. There were black servants who gave you mint juleps. I had never been in the South and it was pretty Southern.

"Chris and Tina grew up that way, so it was nothing new to them. Being in that situation was probably more natural for them than being in a band."

Tina would later remark that David, in his seersucker suit, looked like Gregory Peck.

After the last formality, David, Mary, Jerry, and Linda drove back to New York. Within a week, Talking Heads was back at work on a debut album.

The recording of the Heads' first LP did not go smoothly. Producer Tony Bongiovi and the band had a mutual problem: He didn't know what to make of them and they didn't like him.

Byrne had wanted John Cale, the Velvet Underground veteran who produced Patti Smith and the Modern Lovers, to oversee the Heads' record. Sire was frightened that Cale, a musical and personal extremist, would make an already avant-garde act *really* uncommercial. Seymour Stein said that if Byrne had insisted on Cale, Sire would have relented. But the company convinced the Heads to go with Bongiovi, a fast-talking New Yorker whose current hit was a disco version of the theme from *Star Wars*. Bongiovi, Sire felt, could point the Heads toward, if not the Top 40, at least the FM dial.

According to one source, Bongiovi owed Sire quite a bit of cheap recording time in return for a loan from Stein. Even Bongiovi's interest in the Heads came from an unfortunate angle: He figured "Psycho Killer" as a potential novelty hit. He was in for a rude awakening. Songs about psycho killers just weren't welcome on Top Forty radio.

"They were mismatched with that producer," recalled Ed Stasium, who engineered the album. "I thought the band was great, but I don't think Tony really knew what to make of it."

One witness said that Bongiovi insisted Tina was playing wrong notes on one song. "I've been playing it that way for two years," she replied. "No one else has complained."

It's possible that Bongiovi, like many mainstream pop producers of the time, assessed spare or skewed instrumentation as merely evidence of bad technique. Conventional studio technicians were not often attuned to the frequently raw, "let's-try-it-on" esprit of the punk revolution.

"The strength of the band was in the singing and songwriting," Bongiovi maintained. "The weaknesses were in the playing. They didn't play all that well to begin with. The Talking Heads, for all intents and purposes, was David Byrne. David Byrne was the writer, the singer, and the stylist. You could have taken any other musicians from any band and the songs would have come out almost exactly the same."

Stasium, the engineer, didn't agree. "They were David's songs," he said, "but Chris's drumming and, especially, Tina's bass parts made up the Talking Heads sound. That rhythm section was essential to what the Talking Heads were. Chris's timing was really impeccable.

"Jerry Harrison was more comfortable than the others with overdubbing. It was a new thing for them. Jerry was great at coming in and knocking out the part he had to do."

Bongiovi tried to dress up the Heads' downtown sound.

He brought in Jesse Levy, a Philharmonic musician, to add cello to "Psycho Killer." It didn't work.

"I tried to convey it to him," Bongiovi said. "But he was such a good player that he couldn't make it sound rotten enough."

The real problems between performers and producer began when Bongiovi started pressing Byrne to change his songs.

"David would present me with a song," Bongiovi said, "and it would take forever to get to the chorus. It's always a battle between art and commercial acceptability, and it's a fine line as to who's right and wrong. Some of the choruses were in sections other than what a normal progression for a song would be. I made some edits and changed some parts around."

Some of Bongiovi's editing was done when the band was not in the studio, and he could work without war breaking out. The producer saw this overtime as extra effort to salvage a shaky project. The band saw it as messing with their record behind their backs.

"I was trying to package it in a commercial way," Bongiovi maintained. "Not to make it Top 40, but just to make it so there was a song people could follow. Don't forget that a lot of what I was conveying to the group was input I was getting from the record company. People are in the record business to sell records, and you have to make your music in such a way that people can buy it."

"David would not sing with Tony Bongiovi in the room," Ed Stasium said. "All of his vocals were overdubbed. There was never a confrontation, but it was quite tense."

In later years Tina, especially, would not hesitate to say unkind things about Bongiovi in the press. Bongiovi was, in public, restrained.

"I would never compare myself with somebody as creative as David Byrne," the producer said. "I'm not a good songwriter. I'm just a little technician-type person. I could never conceive of the songs he has. I mean, he is brilliant and I'm not like that.

"He doesn't like me," Bongiovi continued. "I don't know why."

Wondering if David didn't like them was becoming a pastime among associates less culpable than Tony Bongiovi. When Mark Kehoe came down from Providence for a visit, he was struck by how much jealousy, anger, disappointment, and general gossip he heard from the old RISD crowd about Talking Heads. "I didn't feel that way," Kehoe said, "because I wasn't here."

People were still feeling the freeze-out from Chris's and Tina's wedding. Social offenses real and imagined were now multiplying.

"It was too time-consuming for David to spend time with his friends," Jamie Dalglish said. "He was on the road, traveling, touring, getting the albums out. He was driven, absolutely driven, to accomplish this. He deserved all the rewards he got. He sacrificed his personal life for his career."

No one sins for the sake of doing evil, said Aquinas; one sins for an apparent good. Byrne seems to have removed himself from his old friends' feelings for the apparent good of advancing his art and career.

If Byrne's basic loyalty was being questioned by old friends, though, how could one explain his unswerving professional devotion to Chris and Tina?

"Oh, it was kind of like a carnival," Dalglish said. "The carnies all stick together. They don't let the outside world in. There wasn't a feeling of *ego* from David, really. It was more like he had a mission, a do-or-die mission."

Dalglish said he remembered Byrne reading about systems analysis and marketing: "He's a very smart guy. He was always aware of his image and he didn't want to break character. You could turn a camera on him from day one till now and have a great movie."

Dalglish himself would like to have had a great movie. He'd wanted to film Talking Heads' earliest performances, but Byrne said no. "David wanted to be in complete control," Dalglish said. "It was never stated but I got a feeling like, 'Hey, man—this is my thing. Leave me alone. If you want to do your thing, that's fine, good luck to you—but don't mess around with this.'"

Dalglish's greatest surprise came when Byrne appeared at his door one day and took back all the video tapes he'd worked on at Dalglish's studio in Providence. "He wouldn't even let me make copies of them." Up in Providence, meanwhile, Mark Kehoe lost his years of Polaroids. "David just took them," Kehoe said. "I have no pictures of him."

Mary Clarke was finding her boyfriend something less than a social lion.

"We did a lot of things, just the two of us," she explained. "When I think back, it was much more of a solitary thing than I've had with other people. He didn't want to hang around with groups of friends. Maybe because he was with the band so much that he wanted to get away from being with groups of people.

"Even when we went to see the RISD people, it was more at my instigation. A lot of those people were really jealous. They didn't come out and say it, but it made David feel a bit uneasy."

"There was no reason for the band to spend time with anybody else," offered Jeff Turtletaub. "Their worlds were just different. I think it was inevitable. People use people. It's just more obvious when it's somebody prominent. I think a lot of people feel sad. When you see a friend achieve success you think, 'Gee, I'm gonna have a friend who's successful,' And then you realize that, yes, he's achieved success. But he's no longer your friend."

Talking Heads' debut, *Talking Heads: 77*, was released in early autumn of that year. At the same time, Sire released first albums by three hardcore punk bands, the Saints, the Dead Boys, and Richard Hell and the Voidoids. Although the Heads had no more shared musical ground with those bands than they did with, say, Fleetwood Mac, the label decided to promote all four acts with a single punk ad campaign: "Get Behind It Before It Gets Past You!" Talking Heads hated it.

"Because Sire didn't have any money," Jerry Harrison said, "they stuck all those groups in the same advertising. We were really against that. We said, 'Just take whatever portion of that is ours and spend it on just us.' A lot of radio stations got that promotion and just threw it all out."

"To be real honest," Sire's Ken Kushnik said, "That campaign was mostly developed by Warner Brothers. It was the first release we put out through Warner Brothers. It was just a way to promote four records. It would have been a really big mistake to give each of those records its own campaign, because three of them did not have that much to offer. At the time we really thought we were dealing with psychedelic music all over again—a fad."

The sound of *Talking Heads: 77* was thin and nervous, appropriate for David's lyrics and delivery but not indicative of the band's live bottom kick. The album emphasized the Talking Heads' weirdness at the expense of what was most accessible in their sound. The press critics, always grateful for new angles, were kind, and the record appeared second on John Rockwell's ten-best list that year in the *New York Times*. But several radio programmers reacted like the disc jockey at Providence's top underground station, who declared the LP "the worst shit of the year."

"The Warner's promotion guys brought the album to every radio station," Kushnik recalled. "We were told that

David couldn't sing, the band played weird, and that the audience was listening to Kansas, Foreigner, and Boston."

Without radio and with an image as a weird New York punk band, Talking Heads decided that the only way they could attract an audience was to get back on the road and tour. They expanded their northeast routes as far south as Nashville and Atlanta. On December 22, they headed out to do a two-week tour of California.

Talking Heads' first West Coast tour had a significance beyond the obvious merits of extending the band's territory: Now the Heads began selling themselves to local radio stations and record retailers, dispelling their punk-rock image by doing radio interviews.

"The only way we ever got radio airplay was by sort of forcing the issue," Jerry Harrison recalled. "If you go and play in a town, the radio stations feel they should support a local concert. And if you go and talk to them, they at least have to play the record while you're there."

In California the Heads played at small clubs and colleges. They headlined wherever they played, although that sometimes meant small audiences. Most of the California crowd was, by Manhattan standards, a few years behind the times. But the rare punks who did turn up were younger and more colorful than their New York counterparts. While East Coast hipsters all dressed in black, the California New Wavers had the first recorded blue hair.

Soundman Frank Gallagher recalled the amazement of club owners when Talking Heads played under white lights, with no color variations during the set.

"They knew what they wanted and how to get it," Ken Kushnik explained. Tina was handling finances and parceling per diems on the road. "Theirs was very different from the average rock band attitude: 'Where's the beer? When do I get paid? Just tell me when to wake up.'"

On the whole, the shows went over well and David, especially, enjoyed the traveling.

"When we got to the hotel in San Francisco, Chris just wanted to get into a hot bath and David just wanted to get into a car," Mary Clarke recalled. "He drove straight across the Golden Gate Bridge and looked at the view. It was great."

Mary, who felt left out while the Heads made their promotional rounds, was delighted when David suggested that the two of them drive from San Francisco to Los Angeles while the other Heads flew. Tina, however, warned her of one peril: David was still known as a terrible driver. Since Mary, a New Yorker, couldn't drive at all, there was no alternative. "But he was fine," said Mary. "It was really fun."

The Heads returned to New York in time for Christmas, having begun the long process of establishing an identity beyond the usual punk stereotype.

"Very few radio stations played the first record," Kushnik said later. "They went out and toured the country city by city and just won points until all of a sudden somebody woke up and said, 'This record's sold a hundred thousand copies! Maybe we ought to pay attention.' "

Warner's was impressed, and began planning a push for the second album.

When they got back from California, Jerry and Linda moved just across the East River from Manhattan, into a Long Island City loft upstairs from one occupied by Chris and Tina. Tina's brother was a neighbor, and Jerry's old Harvard roommate/co–Modern Lover Ernie Brooks made the place into the Ponderosa of the New Wave. Byrne and Mary were still in Manhattan. They became close with pen pal Brian Eno, who'd showed up from London and had moved into an apartment on Eighth Street in Greenwich Village. Together the three would attend concerts and movies. Says Mary Clarke, "I think David really admired Brian. And I think Brian liked him a lot."

Eno was sensitive, artistic, experimental. After their bad experience with Tony Bongiovi, it was clear to the Heads that this was what a producer should be. Sire didn't agree. If Talking Heads teamed up with Eno, the record company feared, in Mary's words, "They'd make a whole new kind of ambient Muzak record no one would understand."

"The first record had barely come out," Ken Kushnik recalled. "We were dealing with radio people saying it was the weirdest record they'd ever heard, they'd never play it, we could drop dead before they'd play that record. So the Heads said, 'Oh great! Brian Eno wants to produce our record!' I said, 'When the first record goes gold you can have Brian Eno produce the second one.' "

But Kushnik began hanging around with Eno, too, and the Englishman's charm started to win him over.

"I guess back in the deep, inner recesses of my heart," the record executive said, "the parts that haven't been charred off by show business, I wanted to hear that album.

"I knew from talking to them and to Brian that it was going to work. They weren't looking to make a Martian album, they were looking to make a rock & roll record."

The difference, said David Byrne, was that "Bongiovi was oriented toward some preconceived notion of what's commercial, what's a hit, and what sells. Brian's orientation is more toward making recordings he finds pleasing or interesting."

Kushnik also found the Heads a manager, a friend of his named Gary Kurfirst, who'd been working with reggae acts. The Heads were beginning to function less and less as abstract artists and more as working musicians. There was no letup in their work schedule. Before starting work on the second album, Talking Heads had to go back to Europe for twenty-six shows in twenty-four cities in twenty-seven days.

Talking Heads founder and frontman David Byrne. His art-school background and interest in theater and other arts have been the key to the group's development. "None of us is an incredibly gifted musician technically. We each have a style that we're good at. . . . [What we do] doesn't have to be something that's never been done before. But my assumption is that . . . we would do it a little differently." (Copyright © 1985 Kees Tabak/ Retna Ltd.)

David Byrne
5220 Brookway
Columbia, Md. 21044

        Dear
                        I am collecting an "anthology" of
accidents. I would like to eventually publish this collection
when I have accumulated a good number (around 100). So, I
am asking you,   , to write me an <u>objective</u>
account of every car accident in which you have been a
participant. Each account should be about one or two paragraphs
in length. Please concentrate your account(s) on the actual
accident(s) and the events immediately surrounding the
accident(s). If your accounts are hand-written please try
to be legible.

                        If I do succeed in publishing this
collection you will be given credit for your contribution.
Any profit made on this venture will be distibuted equally
amon g the contributors.

                        If you have never been in a car
accident or for personal reasons do not wish to give an
account of your accident, or for other reasons do not wish
to contribute, please let me know.

                        Your cooperation will be appreciated.

                        Sincerely,

                        David Byrne

	Definitely False	Probably False	Probably True	Definitely True
1. Some flying saucers have tried to communicate with us.				
2. All UFO reports can be explaind as either well understood happenings or as hoaxes.				
3. The Air Force is doing an adequate job of investigating of UFO reports and UFOs generally.				
4. No actual physical evidence has ever been obtained from a UFO.				
5. A Government agency maintains a file of UFO reports that are deliberately withheld from the public.				
6. Most people would not report seeing a UFO for fear of losing a job.				
7. The Air Force has been told to explain all UFO sightings as natural or man-made happenings or events.				
8. Persons who believe they have contacted visitors from outer space are mentally ill.				
9. No authentic pictures (photographs) have ever been taken of UFOs.				
10. Earth has been visited at least once by beings from another world.				
11. The Government should spend more money than it does now to study UFOs and where they come from.				
12. Some UFOs have landed and left marks in the ground.				
13. Most UFOs are due to secret defence projects, either ours of another country's.				
14. There have never been any UFO sightings in Soviet Russia.				

During David Byrne's days in Providence, he earned a reputation as being something of an eccentric. This is a page from one of the many questionnaires he would write and distribute to people. (Courtesy Andrea Kovacs)

The band's husband-and-wife rhythm section, drummer Chris Frantz and bassist Tina Weymouth. The pair co-founded Talking Heads with David Byrne in 1974 and later married, in 1977. (Copyright © 1985 Laura Levine)

Keyboardist/guitarist Jerry Harrison had been playing with Talking Heads for six months before officially becoming the band's fourth member in April 1977. Said Tina Weymouth of Harrison, "People who are used to typical rock & rollers have to get used to us. That's why it's good to have Jerry; he gives them what they want." (Copyright © 1981 Ebet Roberts)

Even at the group's earliest shows, they stood out from their punk and New Wave contemporaries. They were clean-cut, wore very typical street clothes, and used only the most basic instruments and lighting onstage. Nonetheless, recalls one observer, "When David performed, he was electric. You could feel the subways under his feet. The keenest statement David made about music at that time was that it could be done minimally." (Copyright © 1977 Ebet Roberts)

In the early days: Chris Frantz, David Byrne, Jerry Harrison, and Tina Weymouth. By now regulars at CBGB, Manhattan's Lower East Side rock club, Talking Heads seemed well on their way. In an interview, Tina recalled the day jobs she, David, and Chris held down. "We kept thinking, 'It's gonna be so great when the only kind of work we have to do is the band.'" (Copyright © 1977 Ebet Roberts)

The Talking Heads during one of their early European tours. During their historic first tour of Europe with the Ramones, the Heads met future producer/ex-Roxy co-founder Brian Eno. (Copyright © 1985 Jill Furmanowsky/ Retna Ltd.)

David Byrne and Brian Eno. A self-confessed "nonmusician," Eno shared with Talking Heads an adventuresome, experimental approach to writing, performing, and recording. Before Eno and the Heads ended their relationship in 1982, he had produced or co-produced three albums: More Songs about Buildings and Food, Fear of Music, *and* Remain in Light. (Copyright © 1981 Ebet Roberts)

The expanded lineup for the Remain in Light *tour, performing in New York City's Central Park in 1980. From left to right: keyboardist Bernie Worrell, singers Dollett MacDonald and Nona Hendryx, bassist Busta Cherry Jones, Chris Frantz (not shown), David Byrne, guitarist Adrian Belew, Jerry Harrison, and Tina Weymouth.* (Copyright © 1980 Ebet Roberts)

In addition to his work with Talking Heads, David Byrne has collaborated with many other artists in different fields. Among his projects are My Life in the Bush of Ghosts, *with Brian Eno, and music for Twyla Tharp's* The Catherine Wheel. *Such exposure has elevated Byrne from the ranks of an ordinary rock star.* (Copyright © 1985 Luciano Viti/Retna Ltd.)

David Bryne performing "Once in a Lifetime" in the film Stop Making Sense. *The film, directed by Jonathan Demme and conceived for the stage by Byrne, was perhaps the most wildly acclaimed rock documentary ever made. If nothing else, it brought Talking Heads' music to a whole new audience and lent the band a certain artistic credibility outside of rock & roll.* (Copyright © 1985 John Bellissimo/Retna Ltd.)

David Byrne in his famous big white suit. "I'll say to myself, 'Look at me. I'm doing something, and people like it.' Sometimes that's surprising. It seems like a surprise that it's me." (Copyright © 1983 Ebet Roberts)

Percussionist Steve Scales, Tina Weymouth, Chris Frantz, David Byrne, and Jerry Harrison at a party for Stop Making Sense. *In mid-1985, the group released their self-produced* Little Creatures. (Copyright © 1984 Ebet Roberts)

One fallout from the success of the 1977 Ramones/Talking Heads tour of Europe was that Ed Bicknell had become Britain's hot importer of American punk acts. This was good for Ed's career but tough on his sensibilities. Bicknell hated punk.

"It was very exciting," Bicknell explained. "I was handling all of the Sire acts, which at the time included the Dead Boys, Richard Hell and the Voidoids, and the Flaming Groovies. One thing I could say about all of them was that they were miserable human beings. Richard Hell was, to me, the worst thing imaginable. Once, upon being introduced to the local girl from Phonogram, he punched her in the face. That was his opening greeting. She just burst into tears. I said, 'What are you doing?!' He said, 'They don't have my records in the shops.'

"With him in particular and with the Dead Boys—I felt sorry for them. There was an element of violence that ran through it all. The audience was quite violent, with the whole pogoing, spitting thing. And going right through the middle of this, in a sort of goldfish bowl, were the Talking Heads. It didn't seem to touch them; they were part of it, but at the same time they weren't. I think it was because they were obviously musically different. They had songs. Everybody else had noise and riffs and spit and gob. They were based on song structures rather than energy, and they had this vaguely intellectual aura about them. They were the Ivy League of punk rock."

For the Heads' second English tour, Bicknell teamed them with Dire Straits, a new, relatively sophisticated London band he was managing. Although the English section of the tour was short, Straits bassist John Illsley recalled, "It was our first time away from home, so for us it was a big deal. The Heads' following was small but it was really strong."

But by the time the Heads arrived in Britain, they were exhausted from a brutal tour of the Continent.

"Whoever organized that tour had them crossing all over Europe," Illsley said. "They'd be driving all night, sleeping in the back of the van. By the time they got to England they were well frazzled."

"They were wiped out," said Strait David Knopfler. "Shellshocked. Basically, David Byrne didn't talk for three weeks. I think maybe he said one sentence, to complain about his hotel room. David just didn't speak. And God knows we were all traveling together in a little microbus. We all had colds together. It was all kind of fast foods and 'Who's got the paper handkerchief?' Whoever's cold was the worst got to sit near the heater at the front of the bus. Tina looked real thin, kind of anemic. Chris and Jerry seemed okay. Jerry seemed the most extroverted of the four. He seemed to be able to detach himself from it all. I think he saw himself as a kind of hired-in professional."

John Illsley described the Talking Heads' sound during that tour: "Chris's drumming was very straight, and David played *jung-jung-jung,* up-down, up-down, up-down strokes, as opposed to more rhythmic playing. But Tina played very melodic bass lines—almost reggaeish on occasion. They were, when we met, a very primitive band, very uncomplicated, which was a great thing to be then. Tina played very simply. That has a lot to do with lack of technique and all the rest, but it also pinpoints the music in a certain way that a funk bass player wouldn't. He'd fill in too much. And because there was no real lead guitar player, she was also playing melodic lead lines. What she did on the bass often made the song. It was very simple and very nice.

"There are so many musicians who are phenomenal, just incredibly talented, that you could look at a lot of bands who play well together and say 'Oh, well—none of these guys can play,' or, 'He's not very good—they should get so-and-so.' That's nonsense. It's what a band does together that's so special."

Dire Straits, a textbook example of a guitar band, changed their strings before every show. They were amused when David Byrne appeared in their dressing room one night and said, "You guys really change your strings a lot, don't you?"

"Well, of course. It's normal. Doesn't everybody?"

"Oh no," Byrne replied. "We only change one if we break it."

The support band was also amused by the fact that Byrne and Harrison often played with five dead strings and one bright. Yet with the Heads' odd, chunky rhythmic style, Dire Straits conceded it didn't seem to matter.

"Tina used to break strings like nobody's business," Illsley said. "She broke a bass string almost every night."

"I play bass much less delicately than David plays guitar," Tina told Vivien Goldman of the British weekly *Sounds*. Tina, who listened to a lot of James Brown, soul, and reggae, played with her thumb.

"It gives an incredible piston action, like fuel-injection fed. I only use a pick for a lighter, faster, more delicate sound. It may not be as punchy or as guttural, but you get these clicking sounds."

"They were really, really good," David Knopfler recalled. "They played everything very fast. Everything was faster than the record. I remember one night Tina couldn't get back out and play. Her hands were falling off with blisters. That was the other time I heard David talk. He said, 'You better get back on, Tina!'

"It was like they were on a merry-go-round and they were so far in, so programmed into kind of *doing* it that I think the conscious process had more or less switched off. They were just saving themselves up for the gig. They'd been four months on the road nonstop, and they seemed pretty whacked.

"They were being treated like stars. Fans were dashing out of the dressing rooms saying, 'I kissed Tina Weymouth!' It was a big deal."

"On the tour they did with the Straits," Ed Bicknell elaborated, "the Heads were being worked very hard. Gary Kurfirst had come into the picture. I'm not saying he was wrong. But it was January, which is quite a cold month in England, and they were doing twenty-four gigs back to back. No days off in a cold transit van. They'd go from Scotland to London and back to Scotland. That tour was the tour they broke in England. You get out what you put in and they were putting in a lot. But it was very hard to maintain that pace and momentum.

"I remember David, on that tour, became, as we say, a little weird. He was starting to feel the pinch of it."

"I think David Byrne had a breakdown in Europe," Dee Dee Ramone said. "I'm not sure, but I think there was a rumor that he had a breakdown."

"This," Ed Bicknell conceded, "was when the turd-on-the-bed incident took place."

The turd-on-the-bed incident has been whispered about in hushed tones for years. According to differing versions of the legend, at London's Portobello Hotel David Byrne became (a) so disenchanted with the service, (b) so bored, or

(c) so whacked out that he did damage to his hotel room, and left on the bed a turd in which was planted a small flag inscribed *For the Maid*.

Some buy the story. Others think it a myth that Byrne, with his desire to be thought eccentric, does nothing to dispel. However, one friend of the Talking Heads who claims to have been in the room at the time declared, "It was hilarious. It was all a put-up job, a scam on David's part."

To the suggestion that there was some question about that, the source whispered, "No, it definitely was. I was there. The band all decided they didn't want to tour anymore at that time. They wanted to have a break. They figured the only way to get out of the shows they had lined up back in America was for David to have some kind of 'breakdown.' So they planned this thing where David would *seem* to trash his room at the hotel. I think he even unscrewed the hinges of the doors. I don't think he actually *broke* anything. I think he just dismantled a few things. Then Tina went to Gary and said, 'David's had some sort of breakdown! Perhaps we can't tour.'

"That was it. They canceled a few days. They were very tired."

Real or pseudowarbler, the result was the same. It was an important moment for the Talking Heads, the moment they pulled free of outside momentum and asserted control.

When they returned to New York, Talking Heads prepared to record their second album.

"David would write songs on scraps of paper," Mary said. "Then he got a typewriter and started typing—all capital letters."

"I couldn't believe 'The Girls Want to Be with the Girls' when I saw it," Tina recalled. "The words were all verbatim from a conversation David and I had. It was real interesting;

David was just getting acquainted with the fact that girls are just like boys: Sometimes it's just reassuring for girls to be with other girls. It's not because they're sitting in a corner laughing at the boys."

In the middle of March the group headed to the Bahamas with Eno to record the second LP. After the tension and hair-pulling of the first album, this felt like a paid vacation. The band got a second crack at some songs they'd attempted and abandoned while working with Bongiovi, including Al Green's "Take Me to the River," the cover that would be their first hit.

"Brian was really understanding in a song like 'Take Me to the River,' " Tina remembered. "We played it live in the studio with David singing. Brian could very easily have imposed himself on that song, because there's so much room for it. But it sounded so great when we listened to the playback that we immediately imposed a rule on ourselves —that this song would have absolutely no additional playing on it, except that we could add one thing: anybody could play single notes. No double notes. You could just play one *ping* or *bop* or *pang*. That was then treated by Brian's synthesizer in the same way the snare was treated—so that it had a delay, an echo. That gave it a real underwater sound. I think it's good because the song is very repetitive, and these little things that happen are not overbearing."

Byrne had been concerned that some people misinterpreted the intentions of some of the songs on the first album. A lot of listeners had assumed from tracks like "Don't Worry about the Government" that the writer had a bourgeois sensibility. He tried to clarify his perspective with a song called "The Big Country." In it, the singer looked down from an airplane on middle America's homes, schools, and baseball fields, noted how pleasant it was, and concluded, "I wouldn't live there if you paid me."

Immediately after finishing the album, the Heads hit the

road for a two-week tour of the Northeast. Then they went back to Europe.

England and Europe had become lucrative markets for Talking Heads, whose popularity in America at that time was limited to the East Coast, particularly Manhattan. The band could go to Europe on sporadic six-week bashes, play to maybe fifteen hundred people a night, and do well enough financially to keep them going for a while.

The Heads' financial incentive for returning to Europe was bolstered by Sire's desire to get them to the Continent for business reasons. The label was switching its European distribution from Phonogram to WEA (Warner's); after the commercial failure of Richard Hell, the Dead Boys, and the Saints, Talking Heads had emerged as Sire's flagship act. It was hoped that a Heads tour would generate enthusiasm with the new distributor.

The timing, however, was rotten. The dates Sire had scheduled were the same dates as Europe's soccer championships, an event that draws more attention on the Continent than a combined World Series, Super Bowl, and presidential election would in the United States.

"I kept saying to people at Sire, 'Don't send them over!' " Bicknell said. " 'They shouldn't be doing this tour!' I told Seymour and various other people it was a complete mistake, but they insisted.

"I met the band in Holland, and they asked why they weren't drawing any people. I told them, 'Every night you play, you're playing against the World Cup Match! It's on TV every night.' Tina was really angry about it. She said, 'I haven't been told this!' "

Manager Gary Kurfirst flew over to keep things cool, but his relations with Bicknell were touchy. Bicknell had heard that he'd been Talking Heads' first choice for management, and he was hurt that his friend Ken Kushnik had instead lobbied for Kurfirst; it made sense, of course, for a New York band to have a New York manager. Bicknell said that when he saw Chris and Tina for the first time after they signed with Kurfirst, they said they'd been told that Bicknell had rejected their management request. Bicknell was shocked. He'd never been asked.

"Kurfirst is a ruthless man," said Paul Cummins, who road-managed those European tour dates. "And I say, 'Full points to Gary Kurfirst.' It's a ruthless business."

Cummins—small, polite, attractive—was the perfect British gentleman, dedicated to his work and capable of shocking those who thought him too mild with sudden bursts of wild temper.

"They were the easiest band I'd ever tour-managed," Cummins said. "They put everything into their music. We had an absolute ball. I loved their music, they're great people, and we got on famously."

The European tour also provided opportunities for audiences to confront the Heads on their music's political implications, or lack thereof. Almost all great rock music conveys a spirit that is independent-minded and antiauthoritarian, and thus, at least implicitly, political. Many pop artists, from Jackson Browne to the Clash, have also aligned themselves with specific causes; while fighting deportation from the United States, John Lennon actually *became* a political cause. Political rock went out of vogue during the early seventies but returned with the rise of punk, particularly the European variety. But while it was easy to identify the sympathies of the Sex Pistols ("Anarchy in the U.K.") or the Clash ("Sandinista!") the Heads typically eluded categorization. Byrne and Harrison were from liberal backgrounds, and Chris and Tina had their military genes, but there's never been any evidence of political friction within the band. Their official line was that they were more con-

cerned with people's sensibilities than with their own plat-
forms or manifestoes.

"Some very stupid kids interviewed us in Germany," Tina
recalled. "They said, 'Don't you know there are lots of
liberals and left-wingers here who hate your song, "Don't
Worry about the Government"?'

"We laughed at them and said, 'Well, we hope they're
not your leaders because they must be very stupid people.'
I think that song is, in fact, very subversive. People who
would be afraid to listen to a song they thought was political,
or a group with a political image threatening to them, will
listen to that song. They take it all in, and they can interpret
it for themselves and say, 'Wait a minute—there's something twisted here, there's something wrong.' But it's left for
them to decide for themselves what it is that's twisted about
the government today. We're not telling them what's
wrong. We're just leaving it open, because the solutions are
not necessarily pat. Solutions have to change all the time
according to situations."

Tina, of course, had her own political side. "Tina was a
very forceful personality," Bicknell said. "She was the one
of the four naturally oriented toward the business side of
things. Of course, through the business side you can ac-
quire power. Power in rock bands comes through two
things: either by being the main creative force or by being
the business head. Now, David was obviously the creative
force in that band, but she is probably the business force."

Rock & roll has traditionally been an all-male bastion, and
women who have cracked the club have usually endured
more than the usual bouts with sexism. But Tina, Bicknell
feels, had a knack for turning a seeming disadvantage into
a strength.

"It's much harder for a man to confront a woman than
to confront another man," he points out. "Most Western
men wouldn't hit a woman or say 'Fuck off' to her. In rows

in all-male rock groups, there are literally no restrictions on what anybody will do to anybody else. People can be hammered with cymbal stands. But put a woman in that situation and you immediately change the atmosphere. Tina is very shrewd at using her feminity. She's quite a tough cookie. And one respects her for that. She's in a rollercoaster sort of business."

"Tina and David had lots of chats all the time," Cummins recalled. "They were getting something straightened out between them. There was a little bit of friction for a little while. If there were ever any discussions to be had, it seems Tina and David had the talks.

"I think Tina's always been the one who supported the band, really. Tina's a very strong person and a very sensible person, too. I think she's wonderful. She had a lot to say and everyone responded to that. Tina would keep David in check. She was certainly a balancing power to keep things on an even keel, because they're all artists; they came from that crazy background. They need that sort of outlet."

Cummins traveled through Europe in a car with the four band members. When there was a break in the tour, Byrne indulged his wanderlust by recruiting Jerry to take off for a quick holiday in France. In London, the World Cup curse was broken when the group headlined at the Lyceum. The Heads had become a very hot ticket, and the hall was jammed. "It was a brilliant night," Cummins remembered. "They opened the roof and it was charged. They were great."

"In a way," Bicknell said, "there was no individual ambition. It was almost a *corporate* ambition on the part of all of them to make Talking Heads popular and to do it their way."

That corporate ambition—identified by friends as "the carnies all sticking together"—was the means toward acquiring both artistic status and financial security, both of which are crucial in the music business. Once the Heads knew they were onto something, they blocked out all distractions.

More Songs about Buildings and Food, the second Talking Heads album, was released while the band was still in Europe. The album, produced with Brian Eno, in fact proved more commercial than its Bongiovi-produced predecessor. The company decided to approach radio again, this time with a record that, for all its "ambience," was much richer sonically and better produced than earlier releases. Radio responded. "Even some of the radio people who said they'd never play it on the air said they listened to it at home," Kushnik said.

Some of the material on *More Songs,* such as Wayne Zieve's "Artists Only," had actually been around since before the first LP. The style of the compositions was not different. What was new was the richness of the sound; it welcomed listeners as much as the first album had pushed them away.

The Heads' constant touring motivated album sales, which spurred radio play on more progressive stations. Here and there, mainstream rock radio outlets began slipping the Heads' cover of "Take Me to the River" into their playlists.

"The fact that it was a cover made it a safer bet," Jerry Harrison said. "If other people at the radio station said, 'What are you playing that new-wave music for?' the programmer could say, 'This is a great old Al Green song!' It had some other credibility."

Getting their version of "Take Me to the River" on the radio proved a small triumph for Talking Heads on another level: Two other covers of the song were released at the same time by more established artists: one by ex–band drummer Levon Helm and the other by Eno's old Roxy Music partner

Bryan Ferry. Beating out Ferry's version was especially sweet, as the Heads suspected the Englishman had gotten the idea of cutting the song from the Heads when they opened for him at the Bottom Line in New York City the year before.

"Eventually 99 percent of the FM stations played the Talking Heads' 'Take Me to the River,'" said Kushnik. "But it was six months from the release of the album until some of the bigger, more tight-listed stations played it. That record broke some ground."

For Talking Heads, 1978 was a great year, but Andrea Kovacs was in the middle of a grand mal bummer. She'd lie in her apartment and hear Talking Heads music wafting up from the room downstairs. It was like a nightmare. All she was trying to do was forget David, forget that he was now with her old friend Mary, forget the guilt and embarrassment—and his voice kept rising through her floor.

She continued to work on her photomontages, her big constructs made from lots of Polaroids. When she saw the cover of *More Songs about Buildings and Food*, Andrea *really* hit bottom. David had used her photomontage style on the album cover. Furious, she wrote him a letter of complaint. Byrne denied that there was any influence.

"All of my friends were saying, 'Look what David's done!' and 'Did you help David with this?'"

Even a skeptic would have had a tough time missing the overt similarities between Andrea's work and the Heads' album cover. If Byrne had been spurred on to stardom by Andrea's mistreatment, he was paying her back with an artistic vengeance that made Elvis Costello look like John Sebastian.

"David would never come out and say, 'I want to do this,'" Mary Clarke said. "It always seemed to me that the band were very intelligent about what they were doing. I always used to say, 'Boy, they have not made one mistake! It wasn't a fast thing. It was just a steady climb.' "

It bothered Mary when the press made Byrne out to be a weirdo, a rock version of Anthony Perkins in *Psycho*.

"I didn't think he was weird," she said. "Here was a guy who would say things like, 'I want to have a haircut like Ralph Nader.' It was *eccentric* maybe, but not weird."

By late 1978, when "Take Me to the River" finally inched into the Top 40, Byrne and Mary were drifting apart. If there was any sort of trauma involved, no one discussed it.

Talking Heads' second album had done everything they'd hoped. They would use Eno, who had become something very much like a fifth member, for the follow-up. The group's success was tainted just a shade by the fact that their hit was the one song they'd recorded that was not a Talking Heads original. "Take Me to the River" had gotten the band past radio's anti–New Wave barrier, but, having made that leap, they would not repeat the trick; the band made sure there were no covers on the third album.

Happy as they were to continue the association with Eno, the band wanted to be sure the new LP would be a step forward, rather than just a consolidation of their earlier success. The new songs were mostly set in minor keys, giving them a darker tone.

"When David started writing he used love as a metaphor for other things," Tina said at the time. "Now it's the opposite. For two years he's been saying he wanted to write songs that are less overtly about love. So now he's using the metaphor of politics or a contract with a record company as a metaphor for a love relationship."

Byrne put it another way: "I don't know that much about metaphors. When I listened to love songs in the past, they'd make you think about other things. They obviously weren't just love songs. The texture of the music made everybody think, 'This is our music, it's different from other music, it's raggedy and jangly and our parents don't like it.' The sound leads people to think about all that sort of stuff, their relationship to the rest of the world around them. So I thought I could write love songs and that it was an easy medium to use that way, but after a while it was too easy . . . you start to feel like you could do something a little more interesting, with a little quirkier subject."

In writing some of the songs, Byrne tried exercises in what he called "nonrational logic." He would begin with a crazy premise and proceed from there as if it made sense. He wrote a song called "Paper" based on the premise that a piece of paper could be the most important thing in one's life, that one mustn't let go of it. Maybe he did mean a record contract, or maybe it was just a way of disguising a song about love.

Listening to Neil Young albums inspired Byrne to compose "Heaven," a folky song about a perfect moment— when a bar band is playing your favorite song and you're kissing. "Heaven," Byrne wrote, "is a place where nothing ever happens."

"David wanted to be a crooner on 'Heaven,' " Tina said, "going back to Frank Sinatra. He wanted to have a song where he could really sing."

That song was transcribed by Jerry into a key better suited to Byrne's Sinatra-esque aspirations.

"Animals" was hilarious—a tirade against subhuman species who "think they're pretty smart, shit all over the ground, see in the dark." As Byrne explained, "I wanted to disagree with the idea that animals are, as Jerry said, noble savages—like the way noble savages are looked upon as living in harmony with their surroundings and with each other.

I thought I'd present a contrary point of view of animals as obstinate beings with lots of problems of their own; and we shouldn't pay any attention to them."

Byrne's most significant new composition was "I Zimbra," his attempt to write a song using African rhythms and "highlife"-style guitar playing. African pop music was beginning to interest him, and in the long run its effect on Talking Heads would be enormous.

So would the sort of collaboration that resulted in "Life during Wartime." The music for that song was developed from a band jam at a Detroit sound check. "David had an idea," Harrison explained. "He played something and I played a slightly different thing. He said to the soundman, 'Can you tape this?' Then Tina started playing this bass part."

"David and Jerry discovered that the chord progression that followed from what I was playing," Tina said, "sounded an awful lot like something they had been working on before. So they started playing an adaptation of that."

In the future, many Talking Heads songs would be born of group jams, and lots of hard feelings would spring up over writing credits for them. "Life during Wartime," for example, was credited to David Byrne alone.

For their second album the Heads had gone to the Bahamas; on the third, they elected to work at home. They brought a mobile recording truck out to Long Island City and cut all the basic tracks at Chris and Tina's loft in two afternoons.

"They just set up their home," said Frank Gallagher. "Rattling teacups and everything. We plugged in, and two hours later we were recording. The songs were all structured by the band. Eno never got into the arrangements. Obviously, as producer he would keep an eye on tempos, but he got more into mood and vibe. They had all the songs down.

They just whacked them down in two days. Eno did his work on the overdubbing and mixing."

"I'll tell you what impressed me about Eno," Tina said. "On the second day we recorded, he recognized that I wasn't feeling so great, and he did the dishes. Brian was working terribly hard and he was not feeling so well, but he helped me out. That really impressed me. Nobody in our band ever did the dishes."

"The basic tracks were recorded very quickly," Eno recalled. "We just recorded in the same way that the rehearsals had been conducted. Although this meant some sacrifices in terms of separation—thus limiting future options for changing or substituting instrumental parts—we went ahead. After that we continued work in a studio where we began overdubbing and reassembling the tracks. There was a lot of thought and time given to overdubs. Many were dubbed, few were kept."

Some of the tricks used on Byrne's vocals were technological; others were physiological. On "Memories Can't Wait," Eno put Byrne's voice through a space echo and varied the speed of the reverb constantly.

Byrne was having trouble sounding sufficiently zonked on "Drugs," so he exercised until he was out of breath and then recorded the vocal while jogging in place.

He tried singing "Electric Guitar" as if he were mentally retarded. "We told him to re-sing it," Tina said, "because it sounded too retarded. You couldn't understand the lyrics."

Tina brought in her sisters to sing background vocals on "Air." They billed themselves as the Sweetbreathes.

"The last time we sing 'Air,' " Tina said, "we sing very breathy. Here's an instance where Brian Eno used a conventional piece of studio machinery to achieve an unconventional effect. Normally you record without Dolby and then add it. He did the opposite: He recorded *with* Dolby and then took it off after it was recorded, so that it sounded even more natural.

"Right after the girls came out of singing this very breathy thing, the guitars go *'rooowww!!'* It's very sexy. It's a very boyish, tough sound against these very feminine, ethereal voices."

During recording, Tina said, Eno and Chris were very relaxed, Harrison and Byrne very nervous: their typical natures.

"Jerry was always falling asleep in the studio," Tina offered. "That's a sign of extreme emotional excitement."

Byrne had read a book called *Music and the Brain.* He was struck by this passage:

"The patient was admitted to the hospital and, with her express permission, submitted herself to the hazards of musical influence. My then-assistant brought along his record player and several examples of dance band music were tried out. The patient assured us that none of these was the sort likely to bring on an attack. Finally the assistant produced his most serious recording, which was Tchaikovsky's piece 'Valse de Fleurs,' played by the Orchestra of the Berlin State Opera. Not many bars elapsed before the patient began to look distressed. Gradually she developed a seizure with generalized convulsive movements, frothing at the lips, and cyonosis. As the attack wore off, her plantar responses altered from being flexor to extensor in type. The patient subsequently told me, 'That's the sort of music which always brings on an attack.'"

Byrne decided to call the new album *Fear of Music.*

Maybe it was all the minor keys, but some negative vibrations emanated from *Fear of Music.* The division of composer's credits started becoming a sore point. Although Harrison, Tina, and Chris felt they'd helped write the music for "Life during Wartime" at that Detroit sound check (or, in Jerry's case, even earlier), the album credits read, as usual, *All selections written by David Byrne.*

What really raised his bandmates' eyebrows, though, was the credit on Byrne's African highlife number: "'I Zimbra' was written by the band brainstorming," Tina said. "David had a little riff, and we added on riffs. We rewrote the song about thirty times. We put it into an organization that made sense. Then, on the album, it says, *Written by David Byrne, Brian Eno, and this dadaist poet* [H. Ball]. Actually the dadaist poet wrote the words, and Brian and David figured out how to sing it to the music, but all the music was written by the whole band. Everybody's name should be on it."

Tina said the reason it didn't happen was "because David wrote out the liner notes."

Jerry Harrison was getting a little down because his musical contributions were being overlooked by press and public. Harrison was paying the price of being the man who did everything—no one was sure which parts were his. People credited his guitar parts to Byrne and his synthesizer parts to Eno.

While *Fear of Music* was climbing the charts, Harrison mentioned that he was, after all, a last-minute addition to Talking Heads.

"They'd gotten to know one another over a long period of time," he said. "By the time I joined, I felt like an outsider in certain ways. I still feel like I have to be careful about certain things, because they're prehistory. If there's a disagreement between David, Chris, and Tina, I try not to get involved, because I feel like I'm treading in a direction that I don't know enough about."

Pretty soon radios were blasting "Life during Wartime." Mary Clarke laughed when she heard the line about stocking up groceries and peanut butter; it really sounded just like

David. The Baltimore friends could hear in the song the spirit of their old joke: "Sure is cold today. Must be because of the atom bomb."

Other old friends—people from what Harrison called pre-history—saw a literal truth in that song's chorus:

> This ain't no party, this ain't no disco
> This ain't no fooling around.
> This ain't the Mudd Club or CBGB,
> I ain't got time for that now.

With *Fear of Music* completed, Talking Heads went to play in New Zealand, where their second album had been certified gold.

"We thought," Frank Gallagher said, "what are we going to *New Zealand* for?' We got off the airplane and it was incredible, we were treated like royalty! They sold out the biggest dates in New Zealand, just off the boat. The kids knew all the words to the songs!"

Gallagher's bullheadedness fit in well with the band's work ethic. With two others, Gallagher loaded the truck, set up the stage, mixed the sound, and made sure there was beer in the dressing rooms. "Everyone had four jobs," he explained. "I believe a band should work—babysitter, room service are all bollix. The Talking Heads all like to work. I think they had the attitude, 'It's better than CBGB.'"

Part of the Talking Heads' success as a live act was owed to Gallagher's insistence, from the very beginning, on a fat rock & roll sound. He beefed up the drums and bass, pushing the rhythm in the audience's face. In the early days, this met with some resistance from Sire's Ken Kushnik, who thought the focus should be on Byrne. But however they wanted the records to sound, Gallagher insisted on shaking the rafters live. It was, the soundman admitted, "fascism."

"You gotta make the sons-of-bitches feel it," Gallagher said. "You just can't be quiet!"

"I was a ruthless little boy when it came to doing my job," he added. "Nothing ever got in the way of making the band sound good."

Talking Heads stopped in Hawaii on their way home. Chris had hit upon a way to avoid the endless hassles rock stars faced at the hands of international customs agents. When asked to list his occupation on landing cards, he wrote *concert musician*. While not totally accurate, the designation evoked courtesy and respect in immigration authorities. And you couldn't arrest someone for playing with semantics.

Chris, feeling relaxed and tropical, left the hotel to take a stroll down Waikiki Beach. Talking Heads were now finding fans recognizing them all over the world, so when a teenage boy approached Chris and asked if the drummer would share a smoke with him, Chris agreed as readily as Roy Rogers would pass the canteen to a little buckaroo.

The kid suggested he and Chris duck behind a nearby wall, and as soon as they did the kid's larger pal—no fan of Talking Heads—produced a knife and took the drummer's wallet as a souvenir.

It was a valuable lesson for the most amiable Head. He reported the incident to the police and the band proceeded on to California.

Once there, the hotel phone rang and Chris, groggy, heard a voice identify himself as an officer attached to "Hawaii Five-O." The thief had been captured trying to use the drummer's American Express Card. Chris declined an offer to fly out to testify at Hawaii's expense. He was content to let justice triumph without tossing in revenge.

.   .   .

When the tour got to Providence, Talking Heads played a homecoming show that turned into an all-night celebration. Old Motels Rudy Cheeks and Dan Gosch hijacked Byrne as soon as he was off stage and took him to Leo's, the old RISD hangout where he'd once told Naomi he was going to try computer dating. Leo's now boasted a Dan Gosch portrait of Byrne. While David was hanging out with the artists, Tina, Chris, and Jerry were heading in a white Rolls-Royce to Lupo's, a bar they'd played in their struggling days, and from there to the east side mansion of the Banzini Brothers, a trio of counterculture concert promoters. The Banzini party grew increasingly wild as the night wore on, the hi-fi got louder, and more and more café society guests squeezed in. The San Francisco band Pearl Harbor and the Explosions made their way there, as did CBGB veteran Willy DeVille. Old pals the Talking Heads had never seen before emerged from the woodwork.

Chris was cornered by a local New Wave musician who, in his intoxicated enthusiasm, began comparing his own band's Providence success to Talking Heads' accomplishments. The eternal Southern gentleman, Chris nodded his head amiably and agreed that the two of them sure were in the same game and on the same wavelength.

"Where are you guys playing tomorrow?" the drunk asked.

Chris mentioned Lenox, Massachusetts, a town three hours away.

"Oh boy, I'd love to go. You guys are my favorites. But I'm sure it's too late to get tickets."

"Well," Chris replied sympathetically, "I'll leave a ticket in your name."

"Oh, that's so great, man! Listen, I'll probably get into town a little early. Where will you be staying?"

Chris told him the name of the hotel.

"Great. I'll come by. Now, I might be a little hungry. Can I hit you up for a sandwich?"

Chris smiled and nodded. No problem.

"Just one other thing," said the drunk. "I'll need a way to get up there. How are you guys traveling?"

"Ah," Chris explained, "we're pretty much full up."

The drunk wandered off, accosting other guests and soliciting transport for the hegira to Lenox.

As rock veterans know, it's hard enough for band members to maintain friendships through the travails of tours and making records; that Chris and Tina can keep a marriage going is quite an accomplishment. But then Chris Frantz, everyone seems to agree, is a genuinely nice guy. If he's rarely quoted at length in interviews, it's because he generally sits back and smiles while Tina does the talking. But those close to the band say that, despite appearances, Chris is not a passive partner in Talking Heads and that Tina does not automatically get his vote in band controversies. If Chris thinks Tina is wrong, he will side against her. The outside world, though, will never see evidence of that sort of marital dissension. Chris is a gentleman.

"The only time Tina and I get on each other's nerves," Chris Frantz said after the tour, "is when we haven't gotten enough sleep. We share a room, so I have to wait for her, or she has to wait for me, to get out of the bathroom. Sometimes we get a little edgy or cranky."

Back when he was living in Providence, Byrne had tape-recorded TV game shows and transcribed them. What amazed those to whom he showed them was how much of the footage described the prizes (which announcers reeled off very quickly on the air) and how little of the dialogue turned out to involve the games.

Now Byrne was tape-recording radio evangelists, finding,

he claimed, their passion remarkable. At the same time both Byrne and Eno were continuing the African explorations first apparent on "I Zimbra." They read about African music and culture. Eno even visited Africa. Byrne got a kick out of mixing his tapes of radio evangelists together with African rhythms to make a kind of rap music for WASPs.

He and Eno decided to collaborate, without the other Talking Heads, on an experimental African/electronic album using these and other "found vocals." They came across a book called *My Life in the Bush of Ghosts* by the African writer Amos Tutuola, a narrative about a wanderer who encounters the spirits of many towns and tribes. Byrne and Eno decided the novel's title should also be the title of their new album. Later on, they read the book.

Meanwhile, Tina decided she wanted to take some lessons in funk bass playing. She asked Kurfirst to recommend a teacher, and he suggested his former client Busta Cherry Jones. It turned out to be a very propitious arrangement.

"I taught her how to play octaves," Busta said. "Rhythm and blues players play electric bass within the octaves. It's not walking, it's not patterns going in and out of different chords. It's just bottom, it's the octaves. Tina didn't really have a sense for that; she was trying to be a melodic player, and unless you're schooled in that, it's hard to get into. So I put her onto simple rhythm and blues bass. I was trying to show her how to get the most out of what she knew how to do, get the max out of it."

Just after Busta met Tina, he also met Byrne through his old friend Brian Eno. Busta had played on Eno's first solo album, *Here Come the Warm Jets*, in 1973. Eno had just started working with Byrne on *My Life in the Bush of Ghosts* and invited Jones to be part of the project.

Byrne and Eno decided they'd build rhythm tracks first. They recruited Chris to play drums and, with Byrne on guitar and Busta on bass, started recording. In the tribal spirit of their new enthusiasm, Byrne and Eno wanted to keep away from chord changes, building long grooves that would be colored by layering other, interlocking rhythm parts on top of them.

At the time Byrne and Eno gave interviews explaining this African concept to American fans with all the reverence of anthropologists in a new tomb. But Byrne must have known in his Baltimore heart that he didn't have to go to Africa to discover that hung-on-one-chord multirhythmic approach. He only had to go as far as his old James Brown records.

Putting together music in a manner that would creatively engage such diverse talents as Jones, Eno, and Byrne dictated an unusual approach in the studio.

"Brian's not a *musician,*" Busta explained. "He likes to surround himself with musicians who give him what he likes to hear normally, instead of having to push it out of them. Chris is no doubt a great beat drummer, and David has some really wild rhythm when he sits down and plays guitar. Brian wanted the basic tracks cut with just the three of us. Most of them were approached like rhythmic exercises and funk exercises—dance stuff. We'd cut weird things, like sixty seconds of one groove. Then Brian and David took those tracks and injected their wildness. They might take a minute, cut some things out, and then loop it. They'd take a minute of playing and make it a four-minute track."

After the basics were finished, Busta left Byrne and Eno to experiment and went back up to Canada to produce an EP for a New Wave band called the Escalators. He needed a keyboard player and recruited Jerry Harrison.

The Escalators were trying to move their New Wave style closer to Busta's brand of syncopated funk. Jerry had a great time working with Busta on the project, stretching his wings outside Talking Heads. Before long, Jerry would want to bring some of that excitement back to Talking Heads, where he was still in some ways—and in spite of his craftmanship and music contributions—the eternal new guy.

Busta Jones now had the distinction of having been managed by Kurfirst, playing on an Eno album, recording in a trio with Byrne and Chris, being Tina's bass teacher, and producing a record on which Harrison played keyboards.

Back in Byrne's and Eno's Afro-laboratory, *Bush of Ghosts* was all set to go, the record mixed and the sleeves printed, when the estate of the late evangelist Kathryn Kuhlman got wind of Byrne's intention to use a tape of one of her fiery exorcistic AM raptures as the "found vocal" for a track. The estate declined Byrne and Eno permission. So the whole album had to be canceled until an appropriate substitute could be found and the track remixed.

In the meantime, though, a new Talking Heads album, *Remain in Light,* was scheduled and had to be given precedence. *Bush of Ghosts* was shelved.

There were other tensions in the air. Tina thought Byrne and Eno were getting a little too far into their own world. She commented that they were starting to imitate each other, even dress like each other. The press, and Talking Heads' old allies and sycophants, were starting to overdo the bit about Eno being the fifth Head, maybe even the brains behind the Heads. The idea was bandied about that Talking Heads were essentially Brian Eno and David Byrne. The others were sidemen.

"Jerry very, very much wants to be recognized for what he does," Tina said at the time. "Brainless people just go straight toward David because they just don't understand. That hurts Jerry."

When Talking Heads reconvened in the Bahamas to record the new album there was tension, but there was excitement, too. Byrne and Eno's African explorations led to a decision to let the new songs evolve from group jams, in keeping with their new philosophy of grooves first, then experimentation. This was fine with Tina, Chris, and Harrison, because among other things, it meant they'd finally get partnership in the composing. The last album's best song, "Life during Wartime," had, after all, been born just that way.

"I was initially reluctant to produce *Remain in Light*," Brian Eno maintained. "I had been working for some months with David on *My Life in the Bush of Ghosts*, and my mind was still very much in that record. I agreed to work with the band on generating some new material [that is, as an additional musician], but I suggested they find another producer. After a few days of playing together, the band and, in particular, Chris and Tina, requested very forcefully that I reconsider producing the record. I said that I would do it willingly, on condition that they accepted that I would treat it as I would treat my own work—that's to say as a continuation of the ideas I'd been involved with on *My Life in the Bush of Ghosts*.

"I explained as carefully as I could that this would not be a production in the usual sense, that I was only interested in pushing certain musical ideas at the moment and that if I were producing their record I would pursue those ideas there. I believe I could not have been more clear about this.

"The band understood and accepted what I said. They replied that the ideas I had outlined were not, anyway, unfamiliar to them—this was indeed true; they were extensions of what we'd already done on previous records—and that they were in sympathy with the idea of pursuing a rather exclusive objective such as I'd described. They also urged me to treat the album as a collaboration rather than as a simple production, and it was on this basis we proceeded."

If Tina was among those soliciting Eno's involvement,

she quickly came to regret it. Tina claimed that Byrne and Eno had gotten into a tiff during the making of *Bush of Ghosts* and that the bad vibes got worse while the fourth Heads LP was being made. Eno, Tina said, became petulant in the studio.

"Some days Eno would come in in a bad mood," she said, "and he would just lay his bad mood all over everybody. Instead of being businesslike and professional, instead of saying, 'Okay, I leave my personal problems behind,' he brought all that in, too. 'Oh—stomachache!' 'Oh—this sounds stupid to me; I'm going to erase everything except the drums.'

"When David gives orders, all he does is make the whole thing grind to a halt. That's what both Eno and David did by trying to prove they were leaders. They almost brought the whole thing to a halt."

But even though Byrne's experiments could be viewed as self-indulgent, some of the results were quite good. For example, Byrne laid down a strange guitar riff for one track and, after listening to it, added a second. He decided he liked the second better and boosted it up so that it became dominant. Eno hummed a melody, which Byrne liked and picked up on.

As parts continued to be added, Byrne focused on the vocal melody to give a coherent structure to the mutating musical beast. Going back to his *Bush of Ghosts* transmissions, Byrne put together lyrics from the sermon of a radio preacher: "You may find yourself living in a shotgun shack!"

Byrne sang the song while signaling Eno to pull out and add different backing tracks on different bars. When the work was over, they had "Once in a Lifetime."

Byrne's vocal may have been inspired by the radio evangelist, but those few who remembered the Motels could also hear a lot of David Hansen and Charles Rocket ("This is not my beautiful wife!") in Byrne's game-show-host hyperventilating vocal delivery. Of course, Hansen and Rocket may well have picked up mannerisms from Byrne back when they were musicians and he was considered a local nut.

On these recording sessions the Heads were supplemented by Adrian Belew, a guitarist who'd worked with Frank Zappa and David Bowie, and by Nona Hendryx, the soul singer who'd come out of Labelle to build a cult following of her own.

"I think David really liked African rhythms and music," Hendryx said. "It's something he was instinctively drawn to. It was a risk, getting into African rhythms and sounds and being a white person, expressing it as something coming from him."

Generally, criticism of Talking Heads for cultural imperialism—ripping off black music—was short-circuited by Byrne's utter lack of black affectations in his vocals. Obviously this wasn't just imitation. It was a white, Quaker, Scottish/British/French/Harvard/Kentuckian version of African music.

Certainly the Heads were upfront about their sources. Embarrassingly so, Tina thought, when Byrne appended a bibliography of relevant African readings to the promo bio sent to critics with the record. "*I* didn't read those books," Tina told the press.

Having succeeded in recording their African album, Talking Heads were faced with having to find a way to go on stage and perform it.

"I suggested to David that *Remain in Light* could not be played with less than nine people," Eno recalled. "Unfortunately, the idea was initially regarded with suspicion, by Tina in particular, in that it seemed to represent another attempt to dilute the identity of the Talking Heads—myself being, in her view, the first such dilution."

The additions didn't sound like such a bad idea to Harrison. They already had Hendryx and Belew, but they'd need more players to really get that King Sunny Adé highlife groove pumping. Tina credited Jerry, not Eno, with initiating the expansion of the Heads. There may be room for dual credit; it could be that Eno said it first and Harrison actually did something about it.

Talking Heads' decision to expand their sound and incorporate African polyrhythms tapped into a musical lode that, for pop audiences at least, was at once exotic and accessible. More adventurous fans were already listening to import records of the Nigerian bandleader Fela Anikulapo Kuti, who mixed native percussive patterns with jazz-influenced horn solos and guitar funk riffs that, just like David Byrne's, were routed directly through James Brown. By 1983 there was enough groundswell enthusiasm for the Afropop subgenre "juju" that its chief exponent, King Sunny Adé, made a successful tour of America; he led a band that included colorfully robed dancers, a slew of drummers, and a talented pedal-steel guitar player named Demola Adepoju. It's possible that *Remain in Light* helped open the door for Adé and company. In any event, David Byrne had by 1980 clearly anticipated another musical trend that was both hip and commercially viable.

Expanding the Heads from four to nine musicians did have its share of built-in risks. One was that the experiment might not gel; another was that it just might, and as a result the foundation of the original quartet would become shaky —which is precisely what did happen. The Heads were also taking a chance with their audience, though not a big one; clearly Heads fans had supported the band for taking risks in the past, and the basic idea, to push the music into a more danceable groove, had rarely proved to be a turnoff to pop fans.

While the band was finishing up overdubs back in New York, Harrison went down to the Ritz, a rock club, to see Busta Jones's new band. Busta's group included a singer named Dolette MacDonald and keyboard player Bernie Worrell. Worrell had been part of Parliament/Funkadelic, the hugely popular, hugely influential R&B ensemble that centered around George Clinton. Worrell's tightly syncopated use of electric clavinet, a keyboard that can sound a lot like electric guitar, had been a great influence on the development of funk in the seventies.

It was decided that Worrell, Busta, and backup singer Dolette MacDonald, along with Belew and Hendryx, should be added to the Talking Heads.

"It certainly seemed a more interesting evolution," Eno noted of the expanded band, "than that which most groups choose when they want to develop their live shows: adding larger amplifiers, brighter lights, and circus tricks while the music stagnates beneath."

So there'd be Belew as well as Byrne on guitar and vocals, Worrell as well as Harrison on keyboards, another percussionist (Busta found Steve Scales) as well as the drummer Chris, and—the toughest part—Busta as well as Tina on bass.

Rock bands sometimes have four singers, three guitarists, two drummers, multiple keyboards—but never two bass players. There was once a rumor that the jazz fusion band Return to Forever was going to add a second bassist, to hold down the beat while virtuoso Stanley Clarke soloed, but that never happened and it was considered to be just about the most outside concept anyone had ever heard. The bassist's function in a rock or fusion or funk group is to serve as a pulse, a bridge between the drum, whose rhythm it accents, and the chordal instruments. Bringing in a second bass player would inevitably be seen as a slap at the first, even if

Busta Jones hadn't been Tina's teacher, already an acknowledged superior. Add to that the rock & roll prejudice against a woman playing what had traditionally been a man's instrument.

"It was kind of tough," Busta said. "Everybody was kind of nervous about approaching it. David and everybody wanted another bass player to pound some of the funk stuff, the heavy stuff, but it was a delicate situation. But Tina seemed to welcome it! She got excited about it!"

Tina, for her part, said later that she was glad to have Busta on board, that she appreciated his spontaneity. At any rate, the expanded band was officially getting together for just one show, a New Wave festival in Toronto. If the four Heads felt that didn't work out, they could call the whole thing off without embarrassment.

The expanded band played together for the first time at Chris's and Tina's loft in Long Island City.

"It was real exciting to watch that first rehearsal," Frank Gallagher remembered. "It was pioneer stuff. I walked in, and there was Busta and Adrian Belew and Steve Scales. There was great vibes. It was a challenge to them. Some of the people had just been sittin' scratchin' their asses. Some, like Adrian, were on the verge of stardom."

With so many musicians in one room, sometimes trying to play songs that had been arranged for a spare quartet, someone had to act as air traffic controller. The role fell to Byrne. Worrell, however, had much to do with crafting the overall sound.

"It was funny," Busta said. "Everybody's ear kind of shifted to Bernie and made a big wide open gap for him. Once that kind of rhythm was established, everything fell into place. Everybody was so fascinated with Bernie as a funk master."

Worrell, as humble as he was dexterous, played down his

central role: "We were all professionals. We knew how to not get in the way, how to leave spaces." He laughed. "We *bad*, man, we bad!"

On "Houses in Motion" Worrell took the song's underlying Stevie Wonder "Superstition"–like groove and pumped it up till it dominated the arrangement.

"When Bernie played 'Houses in Motion' or 'Once in a Lifetime,' " Busta chuckled, "Jerry would just lay back and look in awe. Bernie played that stuff incredibly."

"They might have gotten a little inhibited," Worrell said of the original four Heads, "because we were kicking, playing so hard, and their ability was not necessarily up to ours. But our attitude was to just help, and they started working harder."

It seems likely that adding so many players—"diluting," as Eno said, the original lineup—made frontman/songwriter Byrne stand out from Tina, Chris, and Jerry all the more. Tina, not surprisingly, saw it a different way. She said, "Getting the new personnel got rid of any leaders. David didn't know how to tell these black people he didn't even understand what they were saying half the time."

The expanded Heads generally did nothing that Sly and the Family Stone hadn't done before. But rock & roll, traditionally a marriage of black and white music, had for eight or nine years been splitting into distinct racial camps, with New Wave at the far white end. Now the Heads reminded —in some cases, instructed—the more narrowminded of punk and New Wave fans that rock flourished when rules were ignored. By rebelling against the rules of the rebels themselves, the Talking Heads were able to march toward commercial viability (black-tinged rock always sold better than New Wave) with heads held high.

The expanded Heads debuted at Heatwave, a New Wave festival in Toronto. Although it was, in 1980, five years since

CBGB had heated up, New Wave music was just starting to break through to a wide audience. Elvis Costello and the Clash were selling albums, and the Police and Blondie were even starting to get hit singles. Some saw the very notion of a festival as antithetical to punk values, but Heatwave was generally viewed as a validation of New Wave's success. It's safe to say that much of the Toronto audience was newly acclimated to the merits of sparseness, simplicity, and musical minimalism. So, the Talking Heads' new image as a funky, technically sharp, and sonically busy ten-piece ensemble was revolutionary. It made the other acts seem suddenly like last year's model. They stole the show.

The ten-piece Heads moved on to Central Park, then through America, Europe, and the Far East.

"They treated us regally everywhere we went," Gallagher recalled. "I think Chris loved it. They all loved it, really. It was done big for us. Everything was positive. It was a pretty happy touring unit."

"When we arrived in town," Busta said, "it was like *the gang*—the Talking Heads movement. All the people came out. Everybody was interested in seeing them. The press were really good to the band. Everybody was really excited about what was going down. All the fans were waiting to hear. Everybody just couldn't wait.

"Adrian Belew had no ego about being the hot guitar player. We were always laughing, Bernie and all of us. It was just a good time. No bad vibes, no static at all."

"David loved to play games," Gallagher observed. "He would vanish at the airport and we wouldn't know if he was on the flight or not. Kurfirst would be looking for him. One place we couldn't find him, we thought we'd left him. And he was on the flight. He'd run up the gangplank at the last minute. We used to laugh. He's got a sense of humor about him.

"I wondered where they could go from here. Any of them could have done anything they wanted. It was wide open. The band could have broken up after that tour. It was a possibility."

"There was no separation between the original four and the new six," Busta said. "In fact, if it was anything internal, it was between Tina and David."

Tina openly expressed her dissatisfaction with David in the press. After the earlier friction about songwriting credits, Tina, Chris, and Harrison had been appalled, on getting their copies of *Remain in Light*, to find on the lyric sheet, *All songs by David Byrne and Brian Eno*, with Harrison also included on one. The record label credited all songs to Byrne and Eno, with two to Byrne/Eno/Harrison. The record sleeves, inner and outer, read, *All songs written by David Byrne, Brian Eno, and Talking Heads*. This last was especially grating, as it separated David Byrne from the Talking Heads, as if the other three were just his backing band.

There were questions about the royalty split as well.

"The impression had always been," Eno explained in 1985, "that I somehow muscled in on this recording and then disappeared with the lion's share of the royalties. I would like to relate what actually happened.

"At the end of the recording there was great confusion as to how royalties should be divided. It was quite difficult to assess what share each person had in the genesis of any piece, particularly when instruments that had been important to the original conception and evolution of the piece had subsequently been replaced by new parts as the piece developed. What was especially difficult was assessing one's own role in the process fairly; naturally, everybody felt their particular contribution to have been particularly important. I had an idea for a way to divide royalties—each person apportions credit to the other four, but not to him- or herself. So, if the composers are called *A, B, C, D,* and *E, A*'s assessment of a given composition would go something like this:

	A	B	C	D	E		
A's assessment	—	40	20	20	20	=	100%

whereas *B*'s assessment would read something like this:

	A	B	C	D	E		
	25	—	25	25	25	=	100%
and C	30	30	—	20	20	=	100%
and D	25	40	20	—	15	=	100%
and E	20	30	30	20	—	=	100%

By this process, each person's contribution has been assessed by the other four members, but not by him- or herself. If you then add these up, you get an overall royalty division (in this case it will be a set of ratios):

	A	B	C	D	E		
	100	140	95	85	80	=	500

Now, by dividing each figure by 5, you attain a percentage figure for the division (20%, 28%, 19%, 17%, 16%).

Eno continued: "It was on this basis (and nobody had a better idea at the time) that the composer's royalties for *Remain in Light* were divided. I still believe that this was a fair system. As regards the credits on the album sleeve, all of the music was written in varying degrees by all of the members of the band and myself. It was therefore fair to include me among the composer credits. However, David, who did, after all, write most of the vocal melodies and nearly all of the lyrics, felt that he too should be individually named in the credits.

"On reflection, it may have been more diplomatic to have listed all of our names, but I don't think it would have been more fair. The formula arrived at was tactless but accurate.

"You have to realize that, even subtracting the irritant of my presence from the situation, this was a band going through an intense internal upheaval. I feel that I became a scapegoat for much of the bad feeling that was generated then, but I also see that this was a way for them to exonerate each other and thus find a way to work together again."

Tina's recollection, not surprisingly, is considerably different from Eno's. "We took a vote and decided we'd all written stuff; all five names were supposed to go on. Then, when the test-pressing cover came back, there were only two names. We raised a stink about it, and David took the blame. About two years later I found out Eno pushed him to do it.

"And we never said, 'The band's breaking up' to each other. The problem went away because Eno went away."

Still, pressures were building.

"When you meet a painter who's been painting a long time," Tina said, "he has a hard time talking, because his thinking does not involve words. But in music, if you're thinking about songs, there *are* words; and though they shouldn't be taken as poetry out of context, because you have to hear the phrasing and the emotion and the delivery within the music, I think you become more concerned with words. And the more you love words, the more power they have—like voodoo.

"I hate to play when I'm feeling sick, because I'm always afraid that when I'm weak like that, I don't have all my powers working for me—not musically, because I can still play; but I think that I'm afraid that certain people out in the audience who aren't really thinking of what it means to do what we do, might think mean thoughts, and those thoughts are transmitted somehow.

"I've had some very close experiences with these things,

and it's very dangerous stuff. It's not something to tamper with, because if you wish someone was dead, and they're more powerful than you, that's such a strong thing to do to someone that you better be damn sure that you're stronger than they are, because if they are stronger than you, they can turn that around, and it will kill you. I don't really want to get involved in this kind of thing, because it's something that I'm only acquainted with in my own personal experiences, and it's real dangerous. Audiences unwittingly can create the same kind of thing; they can make a very famous person quite ill, because so many people are thinking about this person. It can also give this person real comfort, because people are thinking positively about him."

As the world tour progressed, some mighty voodoo started going down between Tina Weymouth and Busta Jones, dueling bassists with Talking Heads.

"Busta's so forceful," Worrell recalled. "That started to get to her. If you ain't playin', you're left behind, cause Busta's *thumpin'*. Tina was still coming up. She didn't have that *banging* thing. And I think that started to work on her ego. She started to feel a little bad about it."

It's easy to see why. Talking Heads had started as a trio, with Tina prodding and encouraging Byrne. Now Byrne was in a situation where, for the first time, if Tina had disappeared it would have made no immediate difference. Even if some people regarded the studio Talking Heads as an Eno/Byrne collaboration, the live band had been the quartet. Now it was easier than ever for the public to see Talking Heads as David Byrne and band. If so many new people could come in without the group losing its identity, perhaps that identity could also survive the departure of a member.

Most musicians, in Tina's place, would have felt uneasy. It didn't help that, according to Gallagher, "Busta wasn't exactly mister diplomat . . . Tina's strong. She's not paranoid. I think it's just distasteful if someone comes in off the street and wants your gig. Even if it's a great gig."

"It wasn't around at all at first," Busta said of Tina's insecurity. "But toward the end I started feeling that. So I talked with Tina one night. I said, 'Tina, I'm not trying to take your gig. I'm really into making my own stuff happen! I'm only here to try to make you sound like a monster! Make your stuff sound real strong!' The double bass songs like 'Take Me to the River' really made her sound like a giant bass guitar. I really meant that. I wasn't trying to take her gig or belittle her in any way.

"She said she knew, and she thought I was being real sensitive talking to her. I felt there was some underlying thing there. I wasn't sure if it was just her being moody, or really feeling insecure. She never really struck me as an insecure person, but as I look back now, I can see."

The tension got to Gallagher when the tour got to Japan. As the band approached a new airport, they encountered protesters decrying the building of the airport on their farmland. Government security was tight.

"They searched us a couple of times before we got anywhere near the airport," Gallagher recalled. "I said to Steve Scales, 'This is like "Life during Wartime."'" They were shuffling in on us with rifles. I quit in Kyoto. It was a combination of things.

"Byrne was beginning to question my abilities. He'd been listening to some of his friends who went to a show in California and said they couldn't hear something or other. He came up to me after the sound check in Kyoto and told me to mix at the level the tape machine was set at. He was tying my hands! It was a little ego-ish, I thought.

"'Tina,' I said, 'this is it.' She said, 'You've resigned three times before!' I said, 'I know.' But it was incredible. These kids were so hip to it—Japanese kids singing the words! I mean, they cried. Such emotion."

With the world tour behind them, the Talking Heads were at the peak of their popularity, and the end of their rope.

When they got back, Chris and Tina headed to the home they had bought in the Bahamas, in the Compass Point complex where the Heads had recorded *Remain in Light*. Harrison recorded a solo album backed by Nona Hendryx, Dolette MacDonald, Adrian Belew, and Bernie Worrell.

Harrison's album, *The Red and the Black*, sounded a great deal like *Remain in Light* by Talking Heads. It was thick funk music, with Harrison's very white, ironic vocals espousing pep-talk values. Unfortunately, the Heads album preceded it into the marketplace, and the public associated the sound with David Byrne. Harrison had finally gotten the chance to step out into the spotlight, but he found himself criticized for *imitating* Talking Heads' sound, a sound that his partisans—including Hendryx, Worrell, and Jones—maintain he was enormously influential in creating.

With no likelihood of a Heads reunion that year and growing rumors that the band was done for, Sire released a live album called *The Name of This Band Is Talking Heads*, made up of performances from different stages in the band's career. But if *The Name of This Band Is Talking Heads* bought time between records, it also ingeniously combined two staples of the pop music industry: the live album and the "greatest hits" collection. By putting the two together and placing the songs in some historical perspective, the Heads called attention to their own process of growth and creativity. The album seemed more a valuable historical document than the "greatest hits" collections of most peers, which looked like easy-money corporate hustles.

Byrne, meanwhile, agreed to collaborate with choreographer Twyla Tharp on a dance production, *The Catherine Wheel*, for which he'd compose and record a rhythmic score. The choice made sense for Tharp, who had made the proposal to Byrne without ever having met him. Within the cloistered world of dance, Tharp was an innovator whose works and dancers reflected her own strident individualism and ferociously disciplined character. For his part, Byrne had long demonstrated his penchant and willingness to break down barriers between pop and other art forms. At the time *Remain in Light* was released, he'd been quoted as believing that his sensibility had little in common with rock & roll. He was still the conceptual artist who enjoyed playing on the tension between seemingly disparate or irreconcilable forms—for example, the *Bush of Ghosts* LP's mix of evangelical brimstone with Arabic and African musical figures.

Beyond that, Byrne, a longtime admirer of Andy Warhol, had always been shrewd enough to use his art world image to firm up his celebrity connections. The Heads' next record, *Speaking in Tongues*, would feature a limited edition cover by artist Robert Rauschenberg. And in 1984 Byrne would be named by *Esquire* magazine as one of 373 Americans under forty who were changing contemporary society —the only "rock" star to be included.

In any event, Byrne was flexible enough to drop his leader's mantle long enough to put his talents in the service of another. The music he created, mostly long, instrumental sections, was composed of challenging Afro-based rhythms that were not typically danceable—"Serious rhythms that made you move your body, but not in a way people are used to doing in clubs," he explained—along with some hi-tech atmospherics more suggestive of his other work with Eno, who helped color *The Catherine Wheel*'s score. Thematically, the piece addresses the estrangement of humanity from the modern world, a familiar Heads topic as well, with focus on such subjects as the family and nuclear annihilation. Byrne believed that his experience with Tharp also represented the "culmination" of his own African experiments. "I can use it when it's appropriate now, instead of concentrating on it so much. I can assimilate some of those things and use them in a more natural way."

In that same year, 1981, Byrne and Eno finally released their primary African experiment, *Bush of Ghosts*, which had been the blueprint for the layered, rhythmic collage of *Remain in Light*. Regarding their ballyhooed African influences, however, both records paled beside Byrne's score for *The Catherine Wheel*. Ironically, this music was relatively ignored by Heads fans, who figured it to be a "modern dance" experiment.

Eno and Byrne jointly promoted *Bush of Ghosts*. If Byrne had made up his mind about choosing Tina over Eno at that point, he gave no indication. Certainly Eno wasn't getting that signal. He told the *New York Times* that he doubted Talking Heads would ever play together again.

"Tina was talking to George Clinton," Bernie Worrel said. "She was telling him she was really frustrated and wanted to do something on her own. George encouraged her. He said, 'Go ahead, find another outlet.' "

The other outlet made itself apparent back home at Chris's and Tina's place in the Bahamas. Chris Blackwell, the Island Records chief who owned the studio at Compass Point, invited Chris and Tina to use the facilities freely. If they didn't come up with anything, it didn't matter.

Frantz approached local musician/engineer Steven Stanley. "Chris decided he and his wife Tina and I should do something together," Stanley explained. "That we should just go in the studio and experiment from scratch. Just do basics, like the drum parts, and then add bass and other parts as we went along."

Stanley was already living downstairs from Chris and Tina at the compound. They began to play together, a loose series of jams, with Stanley on keyboards. Several rhythm tracks —drums, bass, and keyboards—were recorded, then Tina brought in Adrian Belew and Tina's three sisters, the Sweetbreathes. Belew might have been expected. But Tina's sisters, sweetbreathed or not, were a different matter. At that point, the Tom Tom Club, as Chris and Tina dubbed the enterprise, was starting to sound like a complete vanity project.

The Tom Tom Club, however, produced two hit singles, "Genius of Love" and "Wordy Rappinghood." The timing couldn't have been better—artists from Blondie to Prince were beginning to break down the musical barriers that had kept black pop separate from white on Top Forty radio. At the same time, the Tom Tom Club's music was an utterly unpretentious confection, and was appreciated as such.

Maybe Tina's position in Talking Heads hadn't really been in jeopardy, but now, with two hits, she had the voodoo on her side. Eno's speculation in the *Times* that the Talking Heads were finished gave Tina the ammo to force a decision. Eno was out.

Then came a conflict with Adrian Belew, who felt he'd been treated unfairly in the Tom Tom Club deal. He claimed to have written half the material (including the melody line for "Genius of Love," although Steven Stanley denied it) and then to have been cut out with only a token payment. Belew, who had been lobbying for full membership in Talking Heads, brought suit against Chris and Tina. He settled for a better rate. After that, Belew was out.

The Busta Jones question was still up in the air. Busta had proved a valuable addition to the band, but he wasn't the most straightlaced or dependable of musicians. Most important, his presence had become an irritant to Tina. Busta was out.

It does seem likely, however, that at one point David Byrne at least played with the notion of leaving Tina, or Tina and Chris, or Tina, Chris, and Jerry, behind.

He probably could have kept the name Talking Heads. Names like Steely Dan, Roxy Music, Jethro Tull, and Dire Straits stayed with one or two musicians while sidemen came and went. And even without the band identity, Byrne would have had little trouble translating his success into a solo career. Whatever might have been sacrificed financially in going from "Talking Heads" to "David Byrne" would have been more than compensated for by not having to split the pie. But when the chips were down, the carnies stuck together.

If there had been a staring contest between Byrne and Tina, Byrne had blinked first. Why didn't Byrne leave Tina behind as he'd left so many other friends when relationships became touchy or a career jump was available? Certainly the corporate entanglements, the business bonds that Tina was especially adept at negotiating, were a factor. In a mud fight, Tina could have dredged up contracts, perhaps disputed Byrne's right to use the Talking Heads name. Certainly the group's management and its record company were intent on healing divisions and keeping Talking Heads on course. Since Chris was Tina's husband, Byrne could not have expected a band consensus, usually crucial before a sacking.

Furthermore, Tina had never stopped growing musically. It was, after all, the desire to improve on her instrument that led her to Busta Jones in the first place. Byrne could have argued that Busta was a better player, but he could not claim that Tina was lax. Tina had gone from a novice to a stylish journeyman, developing along the way a style all her own.

Ultimately, Byrne may have realized that, no matter how utilitarian his relationships with Chris and Tina had once been, they did share—after all that time, distance, and accomplishment—bonds and obligations to one another.

"I don't know what they 'should' be," Brian Eno admitted. "They are what they are, and all the ingredients of that particular mix make them that way. To ask, 'Could it just be David Byrne on his own?' is rather silly. It's a bit like discovering that a painting you admire is mainly blue, and then deciding to do a copy of it leaving out all the other colors in the hope of thus improving it. If you like the Talking Heads, it is clearly the relationship between all the component parts that is important and unique. Any one of those parts might be interesting alone but it would not substitute for that totality."

The next Talking Heads album, *Speaking in Tongues*, was produced by the band, with all songs credited *David Byrne/Chris Frantz/Jerry Harrison/Tina Weymouth*. It was an outstanding record, closer in spirit to Detroit or Muscle Shoals than to Nigeria. "Burning Down the House" was a hit.

The LP made no attempt to be avant-garde. Talking Heads, by now pros in every respect, navigated R&B, funk, pop, and blues forms with confidence. They no longer needed to justify any musical limits and their method of building songs out of jams and backing tracks continued to yield interesting inversions of common pop styles. It often sounded as if Byrne were trying to fit lyrics that had been written separately from the backing tracks. That's not to say the record had no left turns: Sometimes the shotgun marriages worked, other time they didn't.

Byrne's deadpan delivery—his flattening of the usual accents in words—seemed to free him from a songwriter's ordinary concerns about how words fit musical rhythms (a by-product was his freedom from rhyme). For example, in a Rolling Stones song, the meter of the lyric ("Ev'ry/where ' I/hear' the/sound' of/mar'ching/char'ging/feet'/boy'") matches the song's musical rhythm. The rhythm of the language can be used against the beat of the music to create tension, but it's always a factor. To some degree, the lyric meter can also direct the melody: It strikes the ear as awkward when a line ending in an unaccented syllable—the *-ing*, say, in *falling*—is matched with an ascending note.

By often flattening his meter—not emphasizing syllables —Byrne made his lyrics much more pliable and also made even mundane phrases sound odd or fresh. The effect on such songs as "Making Flippy Floppy" was that the lyrics seemed to sink into the music, to color the sound without assigning literal meaning.

Musically, the band was staying closer to the pop straight-and-narrow than ever before. But on even the most conventional tunes the fills were frequent; instead of short solo lines there were odd studio sounds—electronic washes, booms, aural whirlpools. This approach was not alien to funk and hip-hop, but the Heads were unusually subtle in its use.

In fact, all the innovations on *Speaking in Tongues* were subtle. The meat of the LP was real rock & roll, with no apologies or condescension. With all the lights on, Byrne's melodies were sometimes exposed as weak ("Moon Rocks," for example, and the verses of "Pull Up the Roots"), but most of the material was terrific. Vocally, Byrne had grown remarkably versatile for one of such humble warbling origins. He sang smooth and high on "Moon Rocks," deep and craggy on "Swamp."

Byrne's radio-preacher character had evolved from the uptight WASP of "Once in a Lifetime" to an authorative exorcist. In "Slippery People," Byrne used that persona to launch a gospel-style call and response with a sheepish chorus. "What's the matter with him?" Byrne demanded over and over. "He's all right," the chorus promised, knees trembling. "The Lord won't mind."

On "Swamp," Byrne's character metamorphosed further, into a frightening, half-cracked voodoo man. On that track he affected a deep, buzzing voice a little like those of blues masters Howlin' Wolf and John Lee Hooker, to evoke a gleefully threatening spook. On the tour that followed the album's release, Byrne performed "Swamp" with madness in his eyes, oozing up and down the stage with one leg dragging behind him.

A literal reading of the lyrics for "Swamp" evokes an image of Satan rounding up souls to lead to Hell after a nuclear holocaust. But literal readers of Byrne's lyrics usually miss the point that their real role is to color the music. It's best to say that "Swamp" is a song about menace and leave it at that.

Speaking in Tongues became the first Heads album to sell a million copies in America. In the wake of its success the press focused on the new tranquility in the lives of the Talking Heads. Tina and Chris had become the parents of a little boy, and Byrne was said to be in love. Indeed, *Speaking in Tongues* had closed with an airy, lovely song called "This Must Be the Place (Naïve Melody)," in which Byrne sang:

> Home—is where I want to be
> But I guess I'm already there
> I come home—she lifted up her wings
> Guess that this must be the place
> I can't tell one from another
> Did I find you, or you find me?
> There was a time
> Before we were born
> If someone asks, this is where I'll be

The *Tongues* tour was turned into a film entitled *Stop Making Sense* by Jonathan Demme, the brilliant director of *Handle with Care* and *Melvin and Howard*, warm, good-natured movies about American dreams and ambitions. The concert film—according to the credits, "conceived for the stage by David Byrne"—was carefully planned and coordinated to create an illusion of spontaneity. It was shot on three successive evenings from three different angles, with eight cameras each time, so that a wide range of effects could be edited from the twenty-four possible versions. The soundtrack was redubbed to correct some musical mistakes.

Since Elvis made his first film in 1956, there have been plenty of movies that were simply vehicles for rock & roll icons. In a few cases, such musicians as the Beatles have helped put together movies that are emblematic of particular points of view or that have simply worked as cinema. The concert movie, a relative latecomer to the genre, first came into vogue with the rise of rock festivals, notably those at Monterey and at Woodstock. *Woodstock*'s success as a film opened the floodgates, and in the seventies fans were regaled by a seemingly endless stream of what amounted to crudely edited cinematic fanzines. A few topnotch Hollywood directors have paid homage to favored groups, however: Martin Scorsese's *The Last Waltz*, featuring The Band's last concert, was an artistic and commercial success, while Hal Ashby's *Let's Spend the Night Together*, a film starring the near-middle-aged Rolling Stones, was not. *Stop Making Sense* is the best of the bunch—the direction is startlingly imaginative yet tightly focused; the music is great, as good as or better than a "real" Heads concert; and the band's presence, notably David Byrne's, is altogether riveting.

The movie's structure, which mirrors Byrne's own oddly stylized spontaneity, continually builds from one climax to the next. It opens with a camera following Byrne's tennis shoes to the center of the stage and a galvanic solo performance of "Psycho Killer," in which Byrne, accompanied by only an acoustic guitar and a tape recorder, seems deftly to walk the tightrope between the psychotic and the bemused. For the next number Tina joins Byrne in a duet of "Heaven," a beautiful countryish melody that shows off David's affinities with such traditional singer/songwriters as Hank Williams. The third number adds Chris Frantz on drums, the fourth Jerry on guitar, and from there on the Heads perform as a nine-piece ensemble with Alex Weir (guitar), Steve Scales (percussion), Bernie Worrell (keyboards), and background vocalists Edna Holt and Lynn Mabry rounding out the group. In the first half of the film, each addition to the band generates an entirely new direction in the music; in the second half, the tone is altered by deft cinematography that alternates between flat, *Shindig*-type sequences and dramatic, often ominously shadowed scenes, and by Byrne's own chameleon changes of appearance.

For one song, David dons glasses; in another, he jogs around the stage during an instrumental break; by the end of the concert, he's wearing a surreal, oversize white suit. His dancing, which once seemed merely spastic, here displays an uncanny sense of rhythm and a physical dexterity that's sensual and full of delight; his wit, which ranges from broad mime gestures to more subtle references—a dance with a floor lamp that recalls Fred Astaire's hatrack number—is thoroughly disarming. The result is a movie that never lets its audience get complacent, as each succeeding musical vignette confounds their expectations.

There is more to *Stop Making Sense* than David Byrne, of course. With deceptively simple framing devices, Demme establishes a personality for each of the Heads—down-home Frantz, passionate Tina, serene Jerry—and at the same time gives the impression of the band as one big, happy family. *Stop Making Sense* showcases a band that knows exactly where it's been and where it's going. And it certainly leaves little doubt about who's ultimately in charge, or why.

Stop Making Sense was an unalloyed triumph, an artistic and commercial success. It became a hit on the art house circuit, gaining a new audience for Talking Heads—an intellectual following who would be unlikely to attend a pop concert but who were nonetheless attracted by the Heads' music and David Byrne's wide-ranging conceptual performance. As a musical document for the already committed, the movie was a fine memoir of the Heads' *Speaking in Tongues* tour, from which most of the music on the film was culled. And it helped define a new standard for its genre, as an arty "rockumentary" that really worked.

By 1983, MTV, the cable music network, had become a real power, the equivalent of a national radio station like Britain's BBC. MTV gave New Wave (or the broad, diverse rock style that had grown out of New Wave) the final push into the mainstream. Kids across the heartland of America were beginning to chuck their Kansas and Styx records in favor of fresh styles and wild icons.

Moving into video, and from there into film, demanded that Byrne go beyond his jerky, spontaneous stage manner into a more stylized, more highly ritualized way of moving in front of an audience. So he recruited Toni Basil, who'd choreographed David Bowie, among others, to help him.

They went to UCLA to study film footage of different styles of dance, of preachers, of people in trances. "The movements didn't come from the idea of dance," Basil explained. "They came from an acting point of view."

Basil said that Byrne showed her the storyboard for his first video, "Once in a Lifetime," and she "just played director." In the video Byrne wore horn-rimmed glasses and a conservative suit, bringing his uptight WASP preacher persona to the screen. The ultimate nervous white man, the on-screen character moved stiffly, while behind him African natives performed tribal dances.

The video for "Burning Down the House" hit a similar theme of cultural juxtaposition. In it, people of four different ages and physical types traded places with the four Talking Heads while they mimed the song. Byrne's substitute was a little dark-skinned boy.

Byrne would go into a room by himself and try out different dance steps in front of a video camera. Then he'd call Basil in to check out the ones he liked. "I wouldn't come in and watch him live," Basil explained. "I would watch only the parts of the video he wanted me to see. I felt that would leave him as free as possible. He'd pick ten or twelve movements and I'd tell him which seven worked. He got the choreography credit on the video, and rightly so. I was first director."

The video of "Once in a Lifetime" became an early MTV favorite—also one of the first clips included in the Museum of Modern Art's permanent rock-video collection. And when the Heads released *Speaking in Tongues*, Byrne himself directed a clip for "Burning Down the House."

"The 'Once in a Lifetime' video was the beginning of David's starting to *move*," Basil maintained. "That piece opened it up for him, I think. . . . Dancing in a teenage way probably didn't appeal to him. But he found a way that he liked to move, that made sense to him, and he started using it."

Basil, used to the eccentricities of artists, found Byrne a generous collaborator. He gave her carte blanche to make a video from his "Crosseyed and Painless."

"When some man says to you, 'I'll give you x amount of dollars and don't let me ruin your fun,' " Basil explained, "that's got to be the greatest creature on earth. An artist can't be any more giving and understanding than that. It was his project, his music, and yet he chose to not do anything that might interfere with my creativity. He's a private person, but I think he's an extraordinarily giving artist."

So David Byrne became a real rock star. His face was always there on MTV, his voice was always on the radio. One night when Andrea Kovacs was going by Tower Records, the enormous music store in Greenwich Village, she saw a mob of kids inside. There, autographing posters, was David Byrne.

Andrea pushed her way inside. She wanted to tell Byrne how Buddhism had changed her life, how it might change his. She took out a piece of paper and wrote on it, "Would you like to come to a Buddhist meeting around the corner tonight?" She folded the message over and passed it to someone who passed it to Byrne.

Byrne took the paper and read it. He looked up to see where it had come from and saw Andrea. The crowd saw him look at her and then look at the note. The crowd heard him say, "I'm sorry. Not tonight."

Then he went back to signing posters.

Following the 1983 *Speaking in Tongues* tour, the members of Talking Heads dropped out of public view for a while. After the series of crises that had threatened to break up the band, they'd regrouped and were now basking on a relatively serene artistic plateau. They'd now produced five strikingly different records, all critically acclaimed, and their popularity had increased with each one. David, Jerry, and Chris and Tina had put out individual LPs as well, with generally satisfactory results. Sire released the soundtrack to *Stop Making Sense*, and the album eventually went gold. For so long Talking Heads had avoided the conventional pitfalls that waylaid so many other rock groups on the way up. Now that they'd made it they were avoiding the pitfalls of success—overexposure and burnout.

In spring 1985, David Byrne released *Music from the Knee Plays* on ECM, a series of musical vignettes designed as "joints" between longer scenes in a projected theatrical epic by Robert Wilson entitled *The CIVIL WarS*. It was natural for Byrne to link up with Wilson, whose theatrical vision began in the visual arts and relied on observational, conceptual themes. In one early play, for example, Wilson features a "cat" so large that when it walked across the stage only its legs were visible.

The *Knee Plays* music—for a horn quintet, interwoven with occasional spoken narrative —was quite a departure for Byrne, and the result was suggestive of early New Orleans jazz funeral dirges. (The New Orleans Dirty Dozen Jazz Band was credited on the LP as Byrne's inspiration for the music.) It was also the first music Byrne had actually "composed" for performance, played out on an Emulator rather than transcribed into musical notation, as Byrne does not read music. The narrative sections, recited by David with deadpan intonation, are droll. After *Stop Making Sense*, Byrne said he sensed that people were picking up on his wit better than before: "They can see that I'm not always completely serious or not always completely demented."

A few months later, Talking Heads released *Little Creatures*, the band's first studio album in two years. Musically, the record marked a return to the bare, stripped-down quartet sound of the early Heads—"very conventional songs, except probably the words are a little unusual," as Byrne put it. Some of the LP's songs refer directly to early Heads tunes —the opening riff of "Perfect World" and that of "The Good Thing," for instance. The title song, pushed along by a sinuous steel guitar, underscores the LP's folk-country flavor. And Byrne's lyrics, while sometimes weird, are generally more serene and compassionate than those on any previous album. "Creatures of Love" is a paean to procreative sex; "And She Was," a happy dreamscape; and "Road to Nowhere," an existential celebration spiced with some Cajun-sounding instrumental textures. *Little Creatures* is Talking Heads' sweetest and least pretentious record, and one of their best.

"I call it work," David Byrne commented recently about his music, "but I think I'm lucky in that it's creative work, and it's pretty enjoyable. At times it's hard to separate it from what would be considered fun. I try to be 'new' only in the sense that it's new for me or the band. It doesn't have to be something that's never been done before. But my assumption is that I or we *would* do it a little differently.

"None of us is an incredibly gifted musician technically," he pointed out. "We each have a style that we're good at. More than anything, there's a kind of confluence of sensibilities that sometimes clicks. It's a common assumption, I guess, about most people who write songs that they're speaking from personal experience. And I guess I am. But there's lots of fears and joys I've experienced that I don't think I'd ever write about. They seem much too personal to me."

Sometimes, Byrne admitted, "I'll say to myself, 'Look at me. I'm doing something, and people like it.' Sometimes that's surprising. It seems like a surprise that it's me."

DISCOGRAPHY

1977

Talking Heads: 77 ✓ VINYL
  (Sire)

Uh-Oh, Love Comes to Town
New Feeling
Tentative Decisions
Happy Day
Who Is It?
No Compassion
The Book I Read
Don't Worry about the Government
First Week/Last Week . . . Carefree
Psycho Killer
Pulled Up

Produced by Tony Bongiovi, Lance Quinn, and Talking Heads. Recorded at Sundragon Studios, New York City.

All compositions credited to David Byrne except "Psycho Killer," on which "David got some help from Chris and Tina." David Byrne, guitar and vocals; Jerry Harrison, guitar, keyboards, "second singer"; Martina Weymouth, bass; Chris Frantz, drums.

1978

More Songs about Buildings and Food   ✓ VINYL
  (Sire)

Thank You for Sending Me an Angel
With Our Love
The Good Thing
Warning Sign
The Girls Want to Be with the Girls
Found a Job
Artists Only
I'm Not in Love
Stay Hungry
Take Me to the River
The Big Country

Produced by Brian Eno and Talking Heads. Recorded at Compass Point Studio, Nassau, the Bahamas

All compositions are by David Byrne except: "Artists Only" (Byrne, Wayne Zieve); "Stay Hungry" (Byrne, Frantz); "Take Me to the River" (Al Green, M. Hodges). David Byrne, vocals, guitar, synthesized percussion; Chris Frantz, drums and percussion; Jerry Harrison, piano, organ, synthesizer, guitar, and background vocals; Tina Weymouth, bass; Brian Eno, synthesizer, piano, guitar, percussion, background vocals; Tina and the Typing Pool, background vocals on "The Good Thing."

1979

Fear of Music   ✓ VINYL
  (Sire)

I Zimbra
Mind
Paper
Cities

Life during Wartime
Memories Can't Wait
Air
Heaven
Animals
Electric Guitar
Drugs

Produced by Brian Eno and Talking Heads. Recorded at Chris and Tina's loft in Long Island City with the Record Plant remote truck. Additional recording and mixings: Hit Factory, Atlantic Studios, RPM Sound Studios, Record Plant, New York City.

All compositions are by David Byrne except "I Zimbra" (Byrne, Brian Eno, and H. Ball). No instrument breakdown for the band. Brian Eno, treatments; Gene Wilder and Ari, congas on "Life during Wartime" and "I Zimbra"; Robert Fripp, guitar on "I Zimbra"; The Sweetbreathes, background vocals on "Air"; Julie Last, Brian Eno, and David Byrne, background vocals on "I Zimbra."

1980

Remain in Light
  (Sire)

The Great Curve
Crosseyed and Painless
Born under Punches (The Heat Goes On)
Houses in Motion
Once in a Lifetime
Listening Wind
Seen and Not Seen
The Overload

Produced by Brian Eno. Recorded at Compass Point Studio, Nassau, the Bahamas. Vocals and additional tracks recorded at Sigma Sound, New York City.

All music and lyrics credited to David Byrne and Brian Eno, except "The Overload" and "Houses in Motion" (Byrne, Eno, and Jerry Harrison). David Byrne, guitar, bass, keyboards, percussion, vocals; Jerry Harrison, guitar, keyboards, bass, percussion; Chris Frantz, drums, percussion, keyboards; Tina Weymouth, bass, keyboards, percussion; Adrian Belew, guitar; Brian Eno, bass, keyboards, percussion, vocals; Jose Rossy, percussion; Robert Palmer, percussion; Nona Hendryx, vocals; Jon Hassell, trumpet, horn arrangement on "Houses in Motion."

1982

The Name of This Band Is Talking Heads
(Sire)

1977–1979 Recordings

New Feeling
A Clean Break
Don't Worry about the Government
Pulled Up
Psycho Killer (*Recorded November 17, 1977*)
Artists Only
Stay Hungry
Air
Building on Fire
Memories (Can't Wait) (*Recorded November 17, 1979*)

Produced by Talking Heads. Recorded at various studios.

All compositions credited to David Byrne, except "Artists Only" (Byrne, Wayne Zieve). "Psycho Killer" (Byrne, Chris Frantz, Tina Weymouth), "Stay Hungry" (Byrne, Frantz). David Byrne, guitars, vocals; Jerry Harrison, keyboards, guitar, piano, backing vocals; Chris Frantz, drums; Tina Weymouth, bass, backing vocals on "Air."

1980–1981 Recordings

I Zimbra
Drugs
Houses in Motion
Life during Wartime
The Great Curve
Crosseyed and Painless
Take Me to the River

Production and songwriting credits as on original recordings. David Byrne, guitars, vocals; Chris Frantz, drums; Jerry Harrison, guitar, synthesizer; Tina Weymouth, bass, guitar, synthesizer, vocals, percussion; Adrian Belew, guitar, vocals; Bernie Worrell, clavinet, synthesizer; Dolette MacDonald, vocals, percussion; Busta Jones, bass, guitar; Steve Scales, percussion; Nona Hendryx, vocals.

1983

Speaking in Tongues   ✓ VINYL
    (Sire)

Burning Down the House
Making Flippy Floppy
Girlfriend Is Better
Slippery People
I Get Wild/Wild Gravity
Swamp
Moon Rocks
Pull Up the Roots
This Must Be the Place (Naïve Melody)

Produced by Talking Heads. Basic tracks recorded at Blank Tapes, New York. Final overdubbing and mixes at Compass Point Studios, Nassau, the Bahamas and Sigma Sound, New York City.

All compositions, music by Talking Heads, lyrics by David Byrne. David Byrne, guitar, keyboards, vocals, bass, percussion; Chris

Frantz, drums, synthesizer, backing vocals; Jerry Harrison, guitar, keyboards, backing vocals; Tina Weymouth, bass (referred to on the LP as "string bass"), guitar, synthesizer, backing vocals; Alex Weir, guitar; Wally Badarou, synthesizer; Raphael DeJesus, percussion; Steve Scales, percussion; David Van Tieghem, percussion; Richard Landry, saxophone; Bernie Worrell, synthesizer; Shanker, violin; Nona Hendryx, backup vocals, Dolette MacDonald, backing vocals.

1984

Stop Making Sense
   Motion picture soundtrack   ✓   *VINYL*
   (Sire)   *VIDEO*

Psycho Killer
Swamp
Slippery People
Burning Down the House
Girlfriend Is Better
Once in a Lifetime
What a Day That Was
Life during Wartime
Take Me to the River

Produced by Talking Heads. Recorded at the Pantage Theatre, Hollywood. Recorded December 1983 by the Record Plant Mobile.

All compositions as credited on originally released recordings. David Byrne, guitar, vocals; Tina Weymouth, bass, vocals, synthesizer; Jerry Harrison, guitar, keyboards, vocals; Chris Frantz, drums, vocals; Steve Scales, percussion; Alex Weir, guitar, vocals; Bernie Worrell, keyboards; Lynn Mabry, backing vocals; Ednah Holt, backing vocals.

1985

Little Creatures ✓ _CASSETTE_
  (Sire)

And She Was
Give Me Back My Name
Creatures of Love
The Lady Don't Mind
Perfect World
Stay Up Late
Walk It Down
Television Man
Road to Nowhere

Produced by Talking Heads. Recorded at Sigma Sound, New York City.

All songs by David Byrne, except "Perfect World" (lyrics by Byrne and Chris Frantz) and "The Lady Don't Mind" (lyrics by Byrne, music by Byrne, Chris Frantz, Jerry Harrison, Tina Weymouth). David Byrne, guitar, vocals; Chris Frantz, drums; Jerry Harrison, keyboards, guitar, backing vocals; Tina Weymouth, bass, background vocals. Also (listed as additional musicians) Andrew Cader, washboard; Jimmy Macdonell, accordion; Lenny Pickett, saxophones; Steve Scales, percussion; Nana Vasconcelos, percussion; Eric Weissberg, steel guitar; Ellen Bernfield, Erin Dickens, Diva Gray, Gordon Grody, Lani Grooves, Kurt Yahijian, additional backing vocals.

1986

True Stories ✓ _VIDEO_
  (Sire)

Love For Sale
Puzzlin' Evidence
Hey Now
Papa Legba
Wild Wild Life

Radio Head
Dream Operator
People Like Us
City Of Dreams

Produced by Talking Heads. Basic tracks recorded by Eric
Thorngren at Sigma Sound, New York.

All songs by David Byrne. David Byrne, guitar, vocals; Chris
Frantz, drums; Tina Weymouth, bass, backing vocals; Jerry
Harrison, keyboards, guitar, backing vocals. Also (listed as addi-
tional musicians): The Bert Cross Choir; St Thomas Aquinas
Elementary School Choir, Dallas; Paulinho da Costa, percussion;
Steve Jordan, accordion; Tommy Morrell, pedal steel guitar;
Tommy Camfield, fiddle.

Talking Heads solo records

David Byrne and Brian Eno

1981   *My Life in the Bush of Ghosts*   ✓   VINYL
   (Sire)

David Byrne

1981   *The Complete Score from "The Catherine
Wheel"*   ✓ VINYL
   (Sire)

Jerry Harrison

1981   *The Red and the Black*
   (Sire)

Tom Tom Club

1981   *Tom Tom Club*
   (Sire)
1983   *Close to the Bone*
   (Sire)